THE COMMENTARY OF AL-QAṢĪDAH

شرحُ القصیدہ

یا عینَ فَیضِ اللہِ والعِرفان

از قلم

جلال الدین شمس

سابق مبلّغ بلاد عربیہ و غربیہ

الناشر: الشرکۃ الاسلامیہ لیمیٹڈ۔ ربوہ

Urdu cover title of the book printed by Ash-Shirkatul-Islamiyyah Limited, Rabwah

THE COMMENTARY OF AL-QAṢĪDAH

شرحُ القصیده

The English translation and commentary of an Arabic poem by the Promised Messiah[as], in praise of the Holy Prophet Muḥammad[sa]

Commentary by

Maulānā Jalāl-ud-Dīn Shams

شرحُ القصیدہ

The Commentary of al-Qaṣīdah
(An English rendering of 'Sharḥul-Qaṣīdah')

Written by Ḥaḍrat Maulānā Jalāl-ud-Dīn Shams
English Translation from Urdu by Falāḥ-ud-Dīn Shams

First published in U.K. in 2013

Published by
Islam International Publications Ltd.
'Islamabad', Sheephatch Lane
Tilford, Surrey GU10 2AQ

Printed at
Raqeem Press
Islamabad, Tilford, Surrey

ISBN 978-1-84880-090-8

CONTENTS

System of transliteration .... *ix*
Foreword .... *xiii*
Introduction *1*

Introduction to Al-Qaṣīdah 5

The Qaṣīdah with Translation 7

Commentary of the Qaṣīdah 25
- The Beloved In The Eyes of The Lover 25
- Exceeding All Others in Love 27
- To Show Envy for Ones Beloved 28
- Intensity of Love 29
- To Mold Oneself Like The Beloved 30
- Everlasting Life 33

The Qaṣīdah 35
- COUPLET 1 35
- COUPLET 2 44
- COUPLET 3 45
- COUPLET 4 49
- COUPLETS 5 and 6 52

COUPLET 7 53
COUPLETS 8 and 9 57
COUPLET 10 62
COUPLET 11 66
COUPLET 12 68
COUPLET 13 71
COUPLET 14 74
COUPLET 15 75
COUPLET 16 78
COUPLET 17 79
COUPLETS 18 and 19 80
COUPLET 20 84
COUPLET 21 85
COUPLET 22 86
COUPLET 23 88
COUPLET 24 88
COUPLET 25 95
COUPLET 26 95
COUPLET 27 97
COUPLET 28 101
COUPLET 29 101
COUPLET 30 102
COUPLET 31 103
COUPLET 32 106
COUPLET 33 107
COUPLET 34 107
COUPLET 35 107
COUPLET 36 108
COUPLET 37 108

COUPLETS 38 and 39 110
COUPLET 40 121
COUPLET 41 121
COUPLET 42 124
COUPLET 43 125
COUPLET 44 126
COUPLET 45 128
COUPLET 46 129
COUPLET 47 140
COUPLET 48 143
COUPLET 49 144
COUPLET 50 147
COUPLET 51 148
COUPLET 52 149
COUPLET 53 150
COUPLET 54 152
COUPLETS 55, 56 and 57 160
COUPLET 58 161
COUPLET 59 172
COUPLET 60 173
COUPLET 61 174
COUPLET 62 179
COUPLET 63 185
COUPLET 64 187
COUPLET 65 191
COUPLET 66 193
COUPLET 67 193
COUPLET 68 194
COUPLET 69 196

SYSTEM OF TRANSLITERATION

The name of Muḥammad[sa], the Holy Prophet of Islam, has been followed by the symbol sa, which is an abbreviation for the salutation (صلى الله عليه وسلم) *Ṣallallāhu 'Alaihi Wasallam* (may peace and blessings of Allāh be upon him). The names of other Prophets and Messengers are followed by the symbol as, an abbreviation for (عليه السلام/عليهم السلام) *'Alaihissalam / 'Alaihimussalam* (on whom be peace). The actual salutations have not generally been set out in full, but they should nevertheless, be understood as being repeated in full in each case. The symbol ra is used with the name of the Companions of the Holy Prophet[sa] and those of the Promised Messiah[as]. It stands for (رضي الله عنه/رضي الله عنها/رضي الله عنهم) *Raḍiyallāhu 'anhu/'anhā/'anhum* (May Allāh be pleased with him/with her/with them). rh stands for (رحمه الله تعالى) *Raḥimahullāhu Ta'āla* (may Allāh's blessing be on him). aa stands for (ايده الله تعالى) *Ayyadahullāhu Ta'āla* (May Allāh be his Helper).

In transliterating Arabic words we have followed the following system adopted by the Royal Asiatic Society:

ا at the beginning of a word, pronounced as *a, i, u* preceded by a very slight aspiration, like *h* in the English word *honour.*

ث *th*, pronounced like *th* in the English word *thing*.
ح *ḥ*, a guttural aspirate, stronger than *h*.
خ *kh*, pronounced like the Scotch *ch* in *loch*.
ذ *dh*, pronounced like the English *th* in *that*.
ص *ṣ*, strongly articulated *s*.
ض *ḍ*, similar to the English *th* in *this*.
ط *ṭ*, strongly articulated palatal *t*.
ظ *ẓ*, strongly articulated *z*.
ع ʻ, a strong guttural, the pronunciation of which must be learnt by the ear.
غ *gh*, a sound approached very nearly in the *r grasseye* in French, and in the German *r*. It requires the muscles of the throat to be in the 'gargling' position whilst pronouncing it.
ق *q*, a deep guttural *k* sound.
ئ ʼ, a sort of catch in the voice.

Short vowels are represented by:

a for ——َ—— (like *u* in *bud*)
i for ——ِ—— (like *i* in *bid*)
u for ——ُ—— (like *oo* in *wood*)

Long vowels by:

ā for ——ا—— or آ (like *a* in *father*);
ī for ى ——ِ—— or ——ٖ—— (like *ee* in *deep*);
ū for و ——ُ—— (like *oo* in *root*);

Other:

ai for ى —َ— (like *i* in *site*);[i]

au for و —َ— (resembling *ou* in *sound*)

Please note that in transliterated words the letter *e* is to be pronounced as in *prey* which rhymes with *day*; however the pronunciation is flat without the element of English diphthong. If in Urdu and Persian words *e* is lengthened a bit more, it is transliterated as *ei* to be pronounced as *ei* in *feign* without the element of diphthong. Thus کے is transliterated as *kei*. For the nasal sound of *n* we have used the symbol *ń*. Thus the Urdu word میں is transliterated as *meiń*.[ii]

The consonants not included in the above list have the same phonetic value as in the principal languages of Europe.

Wherever references from Rūḥānī Khazā'in appear in the text, they are according to the edition published in 2009 by Islam International Publications Limited. Rūḥānī Khazā'in is a 23 volume collection of the books of Ḥaḍrat Mirzā Ghulām Aḥmad[as], Founder of the Ahmadiyya Muslim Community.

Curved commas are used in the system of transliteration, ' for ع, ' for ء. Commas as punctuation marks are used according to the normal usage. Similarly, normal usage is followed for the apostrophe.

---

[i] In Arabic words like شیخ (Shaikh) there is an element of diphthong which is missing when the word is pronounced in Urdu.

[ii] These transliterations are not included in the system of transliteration by The Royal Asiatic Society.

FOREWORD

Ḥaḍrat Mirzā Ghulām Aḥmad[as], the Promised Messiah and Mahdi wrote the Arabic Qaṣīdah [lyric poem] in his book *Ā'īna'-e-Kamālāt-e-Islām* addressing the Holy Prophet Muḥammad[sa], expressing his love for him and praising him for his high moral and spiritual qualities, his beauty, his beneficence and the spiritual revolution that he brought about in the lives of pre-Islamic Arabs who were plunged in the darkness of evil and were a decadent society. About this Qaṣīdah the Promised Messiah[as] wrote:

> This is a wonderful and beautiful Qaṣīdah full of literary elegance and fine jewels of the Arabic language, and is written in praise of my master and leader of both worlds—Ḥaḍrat Khātamun-Nabiyyīn Muḥammad[sa]. To write this Qaṣīdah was not possible due to my weak and humble nature—whatever I have stated is from Allāh. The literary excellence, the interesting dialogue, and the fascinating and comprehensive words in which you find uniqueness and rarity are not a product of own effort; but even then, Allāh has given me supremacy over the writers who are masters of the pen, and this is a sign from my God for people of knowledge. I have expressed this matter for the sole purpose that I

> may be rewarded for being thankful, and so that I should not be counted among the ungrateful.[iii]

The Promised Messiah[as] is reported to have said:

> If any person committed this Qaṣīdah to memory, Allāh would bless such a person's memory.

He also said:

> This Qaṣīdah has been accepted by Allāh, and Allāh has informed me that whoever memorises this Qaṣīdah and repeats it constantly, such a person's heart would be granted a deep love for me and for Prophet Muhammad[sa] and I will reward him with nearness to me.

My beloved father, the late Ḥaḍrat Maulānā Jalāl-ud-Dīn Shams, may Allāh bestow His grace on him, wrote in Urdu the commentary of the Qaṣīdah as well as its glossary in 1956 while he was recuperating in Quetta, Pakistan, after a long period of illness. When later he gave a *dars* [an explanation or commentary] of the Qaṣīdah and its explication in Mubārak Mosque, Rabwah it had such an effect on the audience that there was hardly anyone who was not in tears.

The translation of the Qaṣīdah, its glossary and commentary was translated into English by my elder brother, Falāḥ-ud-Dīn Shams, of America, thus my dream of getting an English translation

---

[iii] *Ā'īna'-e-Kamālāt-e-Islām*, *Rūḥānī Khazā'in*, vol. 5, p. 590

published for the benefit of the wider public—Ahmadis, non-Ahmadis and non-Muslims—has been fulfilled for which I am extremely grateful to my Lord, Allāh the Almighty. Thanks are due to Naser-ud-Din Shams, Zahida Shams and Mubasher Ahmad (all of U.S.A.) who helped initially in various capacities to finalise the script. Thanks are also due to Wakālat-e-Ishā'at, Rabwah and Ayyaz Mahmood Khan who extended their full co-operation in making this book ready for publication. Moreover, we are also indebted to Research Cell, Rabwah for checking and providing the full references given in the book. May Allāh the Almighty grant them the best reward for their tireless efforts. Āmīn

Munir-ud-Din Shams
Additional Wakīlut-Taṣnīf, London
28 May 2013

INTRODUCTION

بسم اللہ الرحمن الرحیم۔[1]

نحمدہٗ و نصلّی علٰی رسولہ الکریم و علٰی عبدہ المسیح الموعود۔[2]

اللہ تعالیٰ کے فضل اور رحم کے ساتھ۔[3]

ھو الناصر۔[4]

TWO NARRATIVES

The Qaṣīdah, which I am about to write the explanation of, is written in the Promised Messiah's book *Ā'īna'-e-Kamālāt-e-Islām* in the last part of its Arabic portion.[5] When I expressed my desire to write the explanation of this Qaṣīdah to Ḥaḍrat Mirza Bashīr Aḥmad Ṣāḥib, he narrated the following:

---

[1] In the Name of Allah, the Gracious, the Merciful (Publishers)

[2] We praise Allah and invoke blessings upon His Noble Messenger; and upon his Servant, the Promised Messiah (Publishers)

[3] With the Grace and Mercy of Allah (Publishers)

[4] He [Allah] is the True Helper (Publishers)

[5] *Ā'īna'-e-Kamālāt-e-Islām, Rūḥānī Khazā'in*, vol. 5, p. 590–594

> Ḥaḍrat Doctor Khalīfah Rashīd-ud-Dīn, may Allāh be pleased with him, stated that the Promised Messiah[as] used to say regarding the Qaṣīdah, 'If any person committed it to memory, Allāh would bless such a person's memory'.

Another narration relevant to this Qaṣīdah has been related by the late Ḥaḍrat Pīr Sirājul-Ḥaqq, may Allāh be pleased with him:

> When the Promised Messiah, peace be upon him, finished writing this Qaṣīdah, his face lit up with joy and he stated 'This Qaṣīdah has been accepted by Allāh, and He has informed me that whoever memorizes this Qaṣīdah and repeats it constantly, such a person's heart would be deeply engrained with love for Me and Prophet Muḥammad, peace and blessings of Allāh be upon him, and I will reward him with nearness to Me'.

I considered writing the explanation of this Qaṣīdah almost 30 years ago, but I was never able to begin. Last year during the last 10 days of Ramadan, I was determined and prompted myself to document the meanings of the complex words, but even with that I was unable to begin. In February of this year, I became ill with plurasea and diabetes and for two and a quarter months remained in Mayo Hospital, Lahore. I came to spend the summer in Quetta as per the recommendation of my doctor.

Here, today, on 29th June 1956, or 19th Dhī Qa'dah 1375 A.H., on Friday, I performed two *rak'āṭ*[6] of voluntary prayer and after offering *'Aṣr* prayer, I invoked *Durūd*[7] seventy times upon my master, the chief of the Prophets, *Khātamun-Nabiyyīn* [the Seal of the Prophets], Ḥaḍrat Muḥammad, may peace and blessings of Allāh be upon him, and I have written these few words as an introduction with the intention to write the commentary of the Qaṣīdah. I have determined that every time I sit down to write the explanation of this Qaṣīdah, I will perform two *rak'āt* of voluntary prayer and shall invoke *Durūd* upon the Holy Prophet, may peace and blessings of Allāh be upon him.

I humbly supplicate to my Lord:

> O Allāh, just as You cured Ḥaḍrat 'Allāmah Muḥammad al-Buṣairī, may Your mercy be upon him, from a long illness as a reward for his Qaṣīdah in praise of our beloved Holy Prophet, may peace and blessings of Allāh be upon him, O Allāh, also cure me from my long illness as a reward for writing the commentary of this blessed Qaṣīdah, which was written by a true lover of our beloved master, the Holy Prophet Muḥammad, may peace and blessings of Allāh be upon him. I also pray that You provide me with multiple opportunities to serve Islam, because the real cure and granting of opportunities to serve are in Your Hands. *Allāhumma Āmīn* [Our Allāh, accept this prayer].

---

[6] A cycle of the formal prayer prescribed upon Muslims. (Publishers)

[7] To invoke salutations upon the Holy Prophet Muḥammad[sa] (Publishers)

Now the actual text of the Qaṣīdah with its translation follows and its commentary thereafter.

Humbly,
Jalāl-ud-Dīn Shams
At the house of Sheikh Karīm Bakhsh Ṣāḥib,
Quetta Cantonment, Pakistan.

Note: In this book, wherever I have paraphrased from the books of the Promised Messiah[as], I have not referenced his books. However, whenever I have used his actual text, the reference is given. Most historical accounts have been taken from the book *Nabyoṅ kā Sardār* [*The Chief of the Prophets*] written by Ḥaḍrat Khalīfatul-Masīḥ II[ra] Mirzā Bashīr-ud-Dīn Maḥmūd Aḥmad. In describing the meaning of the difficult words where I have not included the name of the dictionary, they have been taken from *al-Munjid*, the most famous Arabic dictionary.

INTRODUCTION TO AL-QAṢĪDAH

Under the above heading the Promised Messiah[as], wrote the following before his Qaṣīdah:

هذه القصيدة أنيقة رشيقة، مملوّة من اللطائف الأدبية، والفرائدِ العربية، فى مدح سيدى وسيدِ الثَّقَلَين، خاتَمِ النبيين، محمدٍ الذى وصفه الله فى الكتاب المبين، اللهم صلِّ وسلِّمْ عليه إلى يوم الدين. وليست هذه من قريحتى الجامدة، وفطنتى الخامدة، وما كانت رَوِيّتى الناضبة ضليعَ هذا المِضمارِ، ومَنبعَ تلك الأسرارِ، بل كل ما قلتُ فهو من ربّى الذى هو قرينى، ومؤيِّدى الذى هو معى فى كل حينى، الذى يُطعمنى ويسقينى، وإذا ضَلَلْتُ فهو يهدينى، وإذا مَرِضتُ فهو يشفينى. ما كسبتُ شيئًا من مُلَحِ الأدب ونوادرِه، ولكن جَعَلَنى اللهُ غالبًا على قادره. وهذه آية من ربّى لقوم يعلمون، وإنى أظهرتُها وبيّنتُها لعلّى أُجزَى جزاءَ الشاكرين، ولا أُلحَقُ بالذين لا يشكرون.

This is a wonderful and beautiful Qaṣīdah full of literary elegance and fine jewels of the Arabic language, and is written in praise of my master and leader of both worlds, Ḥaḍrat Khātamun-Nabiyyīn, Muḥammad, may peace and blessings of Allāh be upon him, whose praise Allāh has mentioned in His Own clear book. O Allāh, may Your blessings and peace be showered upon him until the Day of Judgment. To write this Qaṣīdah was not possible due to my meek and humble nature, and limited intelligence; nor could my abilities surpass in this area. I could not originate the secrets that are embedded within this Qaṣīdah. On the contrary, whatever I have stated is from my Allāh, Who is my Friend, and such a Companion is He Who is with me at all times, Who provides me food and drink, and when I make a mistake or am misled He guides me, and when I become ill He cures me. The literary excellence, interesting dialogue, and the fascinating and comprehensive words in which you find uniqueness and rarity are not a product of my own effort; but even then, Allāh has given me supremacy over the writers who are masters of the pen, and this is a sign from my God for people of knowledge. I have expressed this matter for the sole purpose that I may be rewarded for being thankful, and so that I should not be counted among the ungrateful.[1]

[1] *Ā'īna'-e-Kamālāt-e-Islām, Rūḥānī Khazā'in*, vol. 5, p. 590

THE QAṢĪDAH WITH TRANSLATION

يَا عَيْنَ فَيْضِ اللهِ وَ الْعِرْفَانِ
يَسْعٰى إِلَيْكَ الْخَلْقُ كَالظَّمْاٰنِ

O you who are the fountain of Allāh's beneficence and divine understanding;
People throng towards you like the thirsty rushing towards water.

يَا بَحْرَ فَضْلِ الْمُنْعِمِ الْمَنَّانِ
تَهْوِىْ إِلَيْكَ الزُّمَرُ بِا لْكِيْزَانِ

O you who are the ocean of the Grace of the Benefactor and Bountiful God;
People flock to you with empty cups in their hands.

يَا شَمْسَ مُلْكِ الْحُسْنِ وَالْإِحْسَانِ
نَوَّرْتَ وَجْهَ الْبَرِّ وَ الْعُمْرَانِ

O you the sun of the kingdom of beauty and virtue;
You have illuminated the deserts as well as the cities.

قَوْمٌ رَأَوْكَ وَ اُمَّةٌ قَدْ اُخْبِرَتْ
مِنْ ذٰلِكَ الْبَدْرِ الَّذِىْ اَصْبَانِىْ

A nation was blessed by having been able to see you,
while many heard of the full moon which has captivated my heart.

يَبْكُوْنَ مِنْ ذِكْرِ الْجَمَالِ صَبَابَةً
وَ تَأَلُّماً مِّنْ لَّوْعَةِ الْهِجْرَانِ

People shed tears when they fondly reminisce of your grace and beauty;
A fire consumes their hearts due to the pains of separation.

وَ أَرَى الْقُلُوْبَ لَدَى الْحَنَاجِرِ كُرْبَةً
وَ أَرَى الْغُرُوْبَ تُسِيْلُهَا الْعَيْنَانِ

I see their hearts are in such anxiety as if they have reached their throats;
I see that their eyes are flowing with tears.

يَا مَنْ غَدَا فِىْ نُوْرِهٖ وَ ضِيَائِهٖ
كَالنَّيِّرَيْنِ وَ نُوْرَ الْمَلَوَانِ

O you who are the sun and moon of light;
You have illuminated the day and the night.

يَا بَدْرَنَا يَا آيَةَ الرَّحْمٰنِ
أَهْدَى الْهُدَاةِ وَأَشْجَعَ الشُّجْعَانِ

O our full moon and sign of the Gracious God;
O the best of all guides, the bravest of the brave.

إِنِّيْ أَرٰى فِيْ وَجْهِكَ الْمُتَهَلِّلِ
شَأْنًا يَّفُوْقُ شَمَائِلَ الْإِنْسَانِ

I find such a glory in your sparkling countenance;
That surpasses all human excellence.

وَقَدِ اقْتَفَاكَ أُولُو النُّهٰى وَبِصِدْقِهِمْ
وَدَعُوْا تَذَكُّرَ مَعْهَدِ الْأَوْطَانِ

The wise chose your company and followed you;
And the truthful relinquished their hearths and homes to be with you.

قَدْ آثَرُوْكَ وَفَارَقُوْا أَحْبَابَهُمْ
وَتَبَاعَدُوْا مِنْ حَلْقَةِ الْإِخْوَانِ

They chose you, and abandoned their friends;
They distanced themselves from their families.

قَدْ وَدَّعُوا أَهْوَاءَهُمْ وَنُفُوسَهُمْ
وَتَبَرَّءُوْا مِنْ كُلِّ نَشْبٍ فَانٍ

They bid farewell to their base desires, and self-indulgence;
They discarded all their material belongings.

ظَهَرَتْ عَلَيْهِمْ بَيِّنَاتُ رَسُوْلِهِمْ
فَتَمَزَّقَ الْاَهْوَاءُ كَالْاَوْثَانِ

When the clear signs of the truth of their Prophet became manifest upon them,
Their base desires were shattered to pieces like smashed idols.

فِيْ وَقْتِ تَرْوِيْقِ اللَّيَالِيْ نُوِّرُوْا
وَاللّٰهُ نَجَّاهُمْ مِّنَ الطُّوْفَانِ

They became enlightened in the pitch darkness of night;
And Allāh saved them from being engulfed in a raging storm of torment.

قَدْ هَاضَهُمْ ظُلْمُ الْاُنَاسِ وَضَيْمُهُمْ
فَتَثَبَّتُوْا بِعِنَايَةِ الْمَنَّانِ

The fury and wrath of the opponents attempted to grind them to dust;

But the mercy of their Beneficent Lord sustained them and they remained steadfast.

نَهَبَ اللِّئَامُ نُشُوْبَهُمْ وَ عَقَارَهُمْ
فَتَهَلَّلُوْا بِجَوَاهِرِ الْفُرْقَانِ

The despicable and accursed of the earth looted all their belongings;
But their faces gleamed upon receiving the pearls of the Qur'ān.

كَسَحُوْا بُيُوْتَ نُفُوْسِهِمْ وَ تَبَادَرُوْا
لِتَمَتُّعِ الْاِيْقَانِ وَ الْاِيْمَانِ

They thoroughly cleansed their souls of all impurities;
And moved forward to gain the wealth of unflinching faith.

قَامُوْا بِإِقْدَامِ الرَّسُوْلِ بِغَزْوِهِمْ
كَالْعَاشِقِ الْمَشْغُوْفِ فِى الْمِيْدَانِ

In battle, they stood with the Messenger in ranks.
Intoxicated in love, they marched forward to the battlefield.

فَدَمُ الرِّجَالِ لِصِدْقِهِمْ فِيْ حُبِّهِمْ
تَحْتَ السُّيُوْفِ أُرِيْقَ كَالْقُرْبَانِ

The blood of sincere lovers was shed under the sword;
Like the blood of sacrificed animals flowing under the knife,

جَاءُوْكَ مَنْهُوْبِيْنَ كَالْعُرْيَانِ
فَسَتَرْتَهُمْ بِمَلَاحِفِ الْإِيْمَانِ

They came to you looted and naked,
And you clothed them with the cloak of faith.

صَادَفْتَهُمْ قَوْمًا كَرَوْثٍ ذِلَّةً
فَجَعَلْتَهُمْ كَسَبِيْكَةِ الْعِقْيَانِ

You found them dirty like a heap of dung;
And transformed them into a piece of pure gold.

حَتَّى انْثَنَى بَرٌّ كَمِثْلِ حَدِيْقَةٍ
عَذْبِ الْمَوَارِدِ مُثْمِرِ الْأَغْصَانِ

And the wilderness of Arabia was transformed into such a garden;
The streams of which are pleasant and sweet, and the trees of which are laden with fruits.

عَادَتْ بِلَادُ الْعَرَبِ نَحْوَ نَضَارَةٍ
بَعْدَ الْوَجٰى وَ الْمَحْلِ وَ الْخُسْرَانِ

The towns of Arabia awoke to life once again;
Leaving the days of death and drought behind.

كَانَ الْحِجَازُ مَغَازِلَ الْغِزْلَانِ
فَجَعَلْتَهُمْ فَانِيْنَ فِى الرَّحْمَانِ

The men of Ḥijāz, who were given to the love of women;
You made them satiated in love of the Gracious God.

شَيْئَانِ كَانَ الْقَوْمُ عُمْيًا فِيْهِمَا
حَسْوُ الْعُقَارِ وَ كَثْرَةُ النِّسْوَانِ

Only two additions had made the Arabs blind:
Wine and women were all that they sought.

أَمَّا النِّسَاءُ فَحُرِّمَتْ إِنْكَاحُهَا
زَوْجًا لَّهُ التَّحْرِيْمُ فِى الْقُرْاٰنِ

Concerning women clear commandments were laid down;
Prohibiting men marrying those who were prohibited by the Qur'ān

وَجَعَلْتَ دَسْكَرَةَ الْمُدَامِ مُخَرَّبًا
وَ أَزَلْتَ حَانَتَهَا مِنَ الْبُلْدَانِ

And you laid waste the drinking places;
And you closed down the drinking of all the towns.

كَمْ شَارِبٍ بِالرَّشْفِ دَنًّا طَافِحًا
فَجَعَلْتَهُ فِي الدِّيْنِ كَالنَّشْوَانِ

Many were those who were given to boozing;
But you made them drunk with the wine of faith.

كَمْ مُحْدِثٍ مُسْتَنْطِقِ الْعِيْدَانِ
قَدْ صَارَ مِنْكَ مُحَدَّثَ الرَّحْمٰنِ

Many were addicted to playing music,
But you made them enjoy the bliss of converse with the Gracious God.

كَمْ مُسْتَهَامٍ لِلرَّشُوْفِ تَعَشُّقًا
فَجَذَبْتَهُمْ جَذْبًا إِلَى الْفُرْقَانِ

Many were those who lusted for perfumed women,
But you made them adore the Book of God.

أَحْيَيْتَ أَمْوَاتَ الْقُرُوْنِ بِجَلْوَةٍ
مَاذَا يُمَاثِلُكَ بِهٰذَا الشَّانِ

With one look you resurrected to life the dead of ages;
Who can equal you in your glory?

تَرَكُوا الْغَبُوْقَ وَبَدَّلُوْا مِنْ ذَوْقِهٖ
ذَوْقَ الدُّعَاءِ بِلَيْلَةِ الْاَحْزَانِ

They abandoned the pleasures of the evening wine;
And embraced the joy of prayers in nights of grief

كَانُوْا بِرَنَّاتِ الْمَثَانِيْ قَبْلَهَا
قَدْ أُحْصِرُوْا فِيْ شُحِّهَا كَالْعَانِيْ

Earlier, they were bewitched by the charms of musical instruments;
They were held like captives who cannot move.

قَدْ كَانَ مَرْتَعُهُمْ أَغَانِيْ دَائِمًا
طَوْرًا بِغِيْدٍ تَارَةً بِدِنَانِ

Their pleasure resorts were their music chambers;
At times they would flirt with women or indulge in heavy drinking.

مَا كَانَ فِكْرٌ غَيْرَ فِكْرِ غَوَانِيْ
أَوْ شُرْبِ رَاحٍ أَوْ خَيَالِ جِفَانِ

They had no worry but the thought of pretty, singing women;
Or of wine and wine pots.

كَانُوْا كَمَشْغُوْفِ الْفَسَادِ بِجَهْلِهِمْ
رَاضِيْنَ بِالْأَوْسَاخِ وَ الْأَدْرَانِ

They were eager to violate peace and order due to their ignorance;
And were quite pleased to live in dirt and filth.

عَيْبَانِ كَانَ شِعَارَهُمْ مِنْ جَهْلِهِمْ
حُمْقُ الْحِمَارِ وَ وَثْبَةُ السِّرْحَانِ

Due to ignorance, two were the major faults they were known by:
the obstinacy of a donkey and the ferocity of the wolf.

فَطَلَعْتَ يَا شَمْسَ الْهُدٰى نُصْحًا لَّهُمْ
لِتُضِيْئَهُمْ مِنْ وَّجْهِكَ النُّوْرَانِيْ

It was then O sun of guidance that you arose on the horizon,
To give them light and benevolence with your lustrous face.

أُرْسِلْتَ مِنْ رَّبٍّ كَرِيْمٍ مُّحْسِنٍ
فِى الْفِتْنَةِ الصَّمَّآءِ وَ الطُّغْيَانِ

You were sent by your Lord, the Noble, the Beneficent,
At a time when evil and vice deluged.

يَا لَلْفَتٰى مَا حُسْنُهٗ وَ جَمَالُهٗ
رَيَّاهُ يُصْبِى الْقَلْبَ كَالرَّيْحَانِ

What a noble man! What a man of glory!
His breath smells like the fragrance of sweet basil.

وَجْهُ الْمُهَيْمِنِ ظَاهِرٌ فِىْ وَجْهِهٖ
وَ شُئُوْنُهٗ لَمَعَتْ بِهٰذَا الشَّأْنِ

The Protector (God) is visible in his face;
And all of his virtues shine in great glory.

فَلِذَا يُحَبُّ وَ يُسْتَحَقُّ جَمَالُهٗ
شَغَفًا بِهٖ مِنْ زُمْرَةِ الْاَخْدَانِ

That is why he is beloved. Indeed his beautiful virtues demand;
That he be adored to the exclusion of all.

سُجُحٌ كَرِيْمٌ بَاذِلٌ خِلُّ التُّقٰى
خِرْقٌ وَّ فَاقَ طَوَائِفَ الْفِتْيَانِ

Of noble character, revered, bounteous, friend of the God-fearing;
He excels all in the field of virtue.

فَاقَ الْوَرٰى بِكَمَالِهٖ وَ جَمَالِهٖ
وَ جَلَالِهٖ وَ جَنَانِهِ الرَّيَّانِ

In excellence and beauty, he surpasses all;
And in glory and cheerfulness of heart.

لَا شَكَّ أَنَّ مُحَمَّدًا خَيْرُ الْوَرٰى
رِيْقُ الْكِرَامِ وَ نُخْبَةُ الْأَعْيَانِ

Without any doubt, Muḥammad[sa] *is the best of the best—*
A man of extreme generosity, the soul and strength of the nobles, the elect among the elite.

تَمَّتْ عَلَيْهِ صِفَاتُ كُلِّ مَزِيَّةٍ
خُتِمَتْ بِهٖ نَعْمَاءُ كُلِّ زَمَانِ

All noble virtues culminated in his person,
The blessings of all times reached their apex in him.

وَ اللّٰهِ إِنَّ مُحَمَّدًا كَرِ دَافَـةٍ
وَ بِـهِ الْوُصُوْلُ بِسُدَّةِ السُّلْطَانِ

By God, Muḥammad[sa] is the vicegerent of God,
And through him alone can one reach the royal court of God.

هُوَ فَخْرُ كُلِّ مُطَهَّرٍ وَّ مُقَـدَّسٍ
وَ بِهٖ يُبَاهِى الْعَسْكَرُ الرُّوْحَانِى

He is the pride of the pious, the holiest;
He is the pride of the spiritual legions of men of virtue.

هُوَ خَيْرُ كُلِّ مُقَرَّبٍ مُّتَقَدِّمٍ
وَ الْفَضْلُ بِا لْخَيْرَاتِ لَا بِزَمَانٖ

He excels all those who were close to God,
Indeed excellence is a matter of noble deeds, and not limited to time.

وَ الطَّلُّ قَدْ يَبْدُوْ أَمَامَ الْوَابِلِ
فَا لطَّلُّ طَلٌّ لَّيْسَ كَا لتَّهْتَانِ

Reflect! The drizzle precedes the heavy rain.
Yet drizzle is drizzle and rain is rain.

بَطَلٌ وَّحِيدٌ لَّا تَطِيْشُ سِهَامُهُ
ذُوْ مُصْمِيَاتٍ مُوْبِقُ الشَّيْطَان

He is the unchallenged archer. His arrows do not miss the target,
They are dead set on killing Satan.

هُوَ جَنَّةٌ إِنِّىْ أَرٰى أَثْمَارَهٗ
وَقُطُوْفَهٗ قَدْ ذُلِّلَتْ لِجَنَانِىْ

He is a garden and I see that his fruits
And clusters have been brought within the easy reach of my heart.

أَلْفَيْتُهٗ بَحْرَ الْحَقَائِقِ وَالْهُدٰى
وَرَأَيْتُهٗ كَالدُّرِّ فِى اللَّمَعَانِ

I found him to be an ocean of truth and guidance;
I found him to be a pearl of lustre and light.

قَدْ مَاتَ عِيْسٰى مُطْرِقًا وَّ نَبِيُّنَا
حَيٌّ وَّ رَبِّىْ إِنَّهٗ وَافَانِىْ

Jesus silently bowed his head, and died. As for our Prophet,
He is alive, and by my Lord, he has met me.

وَ اللّٰهِ إِنِّیْ قَدْ رَأَیْتُ جَمَالَهٗ
بِعُیُوْنِ جِسْمِیْ قَاعِدًا بِمَکَانِیْ

I call Allāh to witness that I have seen his beauty,
With my physical eyes in my own home.

هَا إِنْ تَظَنَّیْتَ ابْنَ مَرْیَمَ عَائِشًا
فَعَلَیْكَ إِثْبَاتًا مِّنَ الْبُرْهَانِ

Look! If you think that Jesus is alive,
Then produce your proof, if you have any!

أَفَأَنْتَ لَاقَیْتَ الْمَسِیْحَ بِیَقْظَةٍ
أَوْ جَاءَكَ الْأَنْبَآءُ مِنْ یَقْظَانٖ

Have you ever seen Jesus while you were awake?
Or has any living man claimed to have seen him?

أُنْظُرْ إِلَی الْقُرْاٰنِ کَیْفَ یُبَیِّنُ
أَفَأَنْتَ تُعْرِضُ عَنْ هُدَی الرَّحْمٰنِ

Look at the Qur'ān how clearly it declares his death.
Would you turn away from the guidance of the Gracious God?

فَاعْلَمْ بِاَنَّ الْعَيْشَ لَيْسَ بِثَابِتٍ
بَلْ مَاتَ عِيسٰى مِثْلَ عَبْدٍ فَانٖ

Know that there is no proof of his life.
Indeed Jesus died as all mortal men die.

و نَبِيُّنَا حَيٌّ وَّ إِنِّیْ شَاهِدٌ
وَقَدِ اقْتَطَفْتُ قَطَآئِفَ اللُّقْيَانٖ

But our Prophet is alive, and I bear witness to his life;
And I have tasted the sweetness of being in his audience many a time.

وَرَأيْتُ فِیْ رَيْعَانِ عُمْرِیْ وَجْهَهٗ
ثُمَّ النَّبِیُّ بِيَقْظَتِیْ لَاقَانِیْ

I saw his blessed face even when I was young,
And he also met me when I was fully awake.

إِنِّیْ لَقَدْ أُحْيِيْتُ مِنْ إِحْيَآئِهٖ
وَاهًا لِإِعْجَازٍ فَمَا أَحْيَانِیْ

I am certainly among those whom he raised to life,
What a miracle! How well he raised me to life!

يَا رَبِّ صَلِّ عَلٰى نَبِيِّكَ دَائِمًا
فِيْ هٰذِهِ الدُّنْيَا وَبَعْثٍ ثَانٍ

O my Lord, always shower blessings on your Prophet,
In this world and the next.

يَا سَيِّدِىْ قَدْ جِئْتُ بَابَكَ لَاهِفًا
وَالْقَوْمُ بِالْإِكْفَارِ قَدْ اٰذَانِيْ

O my master, as I am oppressed, I have come to your door to seek redress,
These people slander and torment me by calling me Kāfir—a non-believer.

يَفْرِىْ سِهَامُكَ قَلْبَ كُلِّ مُحَارِبٍ
وَيَشُجُّ عَزْمُكَ هَامَةَ الثُّعْبَانِ

Your arrows pierce the heart of all enemies,
And your firm resolve crushes the head of the serpent.

لِلّٰهِ دَرُّكَ يَا إِمَامَ الْعَالَمِ
أَنْتَ السَّبُوْقُ وَسَيِّدُ الشُّجْعَانِ

Bravo! O leader of the world!
You rank above all, the bravest of the brave.

أُنْظُرْ إِلَيَّ بِرَحْمَةٍ وَّ تَحَنُّنٍ
يَا سَيِّدِيْ أَنَا أَحْقَرُ الْغِلْمَانْ

Look at me with mercy and grace,
O my master, I am your most humble servant.

يَاحِبِّ إِنَّكَ قَدْ دَّخَلْتَ مَحَبَّةً
فِيْ مُهْجَتِيْ وَ مَدَارِكِيْ وَجَنَانِيْ

O my beloved, my adoration for you has penetrated
Into my blood, heart, soul and body.

مِنْ ذِكْرِ وَجْهِكَ يَا حَدِيْقَةَ بَهْجَتِيْ
لَمْ أَخْلُ فِيْ لَحْظٍ وَّلَا فِيْ اٰنٍ

O you my garden of delight, You live in my memory all the time,
I see your face every moment of my life.

جِسْمِيْ يَطِيْرُ إِلَيْكَ مِنْ شَوْقٍ عَلَا
يَا لَيْتَ كَانَتْ قُوَّةُ الطَّيَرَانْ

My body yearns to fly towards you out of love;
Would that I had the power to fly!

In the name of Allāh, the Gracious, the Merciful

COMMENTARY OF THE QAṢĪDAH

THE BELOVED IN THE EYES OF THE LOVER

The holy writer of the Qaṣīdah (Ḥaḍrat Mirzā Ghulām Aḥmad[as], the Promised Messiah and Mahdi) felt limitless love for the Holy Prophet Muḥammad[sa], who is the intercessor for sinners and is the beloved of the Lord of the worlds. The writer held the belief that just as Allāh is Unique and Alone in His attributes, His beloved, the Seal of the Prophets, Ḥaḍrat Muḥammad Muṣṭafā[sa] was indisputably unique and excellent in his qualities and attributes in comparison to all humanity. None before him could reach his station, nor would anyone be able to reach it until the Day of Judgment. This is the reason that after his love for Allāh, the Promised Messiah[as] possessed the greatest love for the Holy Prophet[sa]. He states in his Persian poetry:

بعد از خدا بعشق محمد مخمّرم
گر کفر ایں بود بخدا سخت کافرم
ہر تار و پودِ من بسرائد بعشق او
از خود تہی و از غمِ آں دلستاں پُرم

After Allāh I am intoxicated with the love of Muḥammad[sa]*,*
And if this be considered infidelity, then by God, I am a great infidel.

Every limb of my body sings the songs of his love.
Lost in his love I have no desires of my own, but am fully sensitive for my beloved.

(*Izāla-e-Auhām, Rūḥānī Khazā'in,* vol. 3, p. 185)

This is also the reason he expresses his love and affection for the Holy Prophet[sa] in the same tone and manner he expresses his love for Allāh. For example, he wrote the following couplet addressing Allāh Himself:

در کوئے تو اگر سرِ عشّاق را زنند
اول کسے کہ لافِ تعشق زند منم

If all Thy lovers were slaughtered,
I would be the first to proclaim the slogan of Thy love.

(*Ā'īna'-e-Kamālāt-e-Islām, Rūḥānī Khazā'in,* vol. 5, p. 658)

He addresses his beloved Ḥaḍrat Muḥammad[sa] in the exact same manner:

تیغ گر بارد بکوئے آں نگار
آں منم کاوّل کند جاں را نثار

If the sword was waged against thy lovers,
I would be the first to sacrifice my life.

(*Sirāj-e-Munīr, Rūḥānī Khazā'in*, vol. 12, p. 97)

EXCEEDING ALL OTHERS IN LOVE

When an individual possesses many admirers, the person with the strongest love will have a greater desire to abandon life itself for the sake of the beloved. The Promised Messiah[as] has expressed this desire of love in the following couplet:

منکہ مے بینم رُخِ آں دلبرے
جاں فشانم گر دہد دل دیگرے

I am looking at the face of my beloved.
If anyone should give him his heart, I would offer him my life.

(*Sirāj-e-Munīr, Rūḥānī Khazā'in*, vol. 12, p. 97)

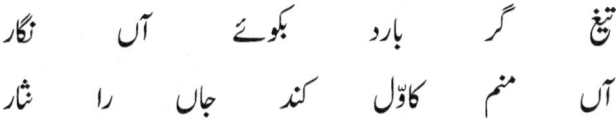

At another place he says:

منکہ رہ بردم بخوبی ہائے بے پایانِ تو
جاں گزارم بہر تو گر دیگرے خدمت گزار

O my beloved, I have come to know of your infinite beauties.
If others are simply your servants, I am prepared to offer you my life.

(*Ā'īna'-e-Kamālāt-e-Islām*, *Rūḥānī Khazā'in*, vol. 5, p. 26)

In the above couplets the Promised Messiah[as] testifies that his love embraces the forefront of all others who claim to love his beloved, the Holy Prophet Muḥammad[sa].

TO SHOW ENVY FOR ONES BELOVED

Due to his extreme love the Promised Messiah[as] could not tolerate hearing a single word against the honour of his beloved. This would deeply offend his heart and soul. His following expression was written in relation to the absurdity and effrontery undertaken against the Holy Prophet Muḥammad[sa] by the blind and belligerent Christian priests:

اللہ تعالیٰ کی قسم اگر میرے سب لڑکے، بچے اور پوتے میرے انصار اور خدام میرے
سامنے قتل کر دیئے جاتے اور میرے ہاتھ اور پاؤں کاٹ دیئے جاتے اور میری

آنکھوں کی پتلیاں نکال دی جاتیں اور میں اپنی تمام مرادوں سے محروم کر دیا جاتا تو یہ
سب کچھ مجھ پر ان کے اس توہین آمیز استہزاء سے زیادہ شاق نہ گزرتا۔

> I swear by Allāh that if all my sons, my grandsons, my helpers and my servants were slaughtered in my presence; and my hands and feet severed, my eyes plucked out and all my desires were left unfulfilled; it would all be less shocking to me than the insult and ridicule of these people.
>
> (*Ā'īna'-e-Kamālāt-e-Islām, Rūḥānī Khazā'in*, vol. 5, p. 15, translated from Arabic)

On one occasion, the Promised Messiah was staying at Lahore, India (currently in Pakistan). Pundit Lekh Rām, a Hindu who used to abuse the Holy Prophet Muḥammad[sa] with foul language, offered *salām* [i.e. greeting of 'peace'] to him, but he did not respond. The Pundit offered his *salām* a second time and he still paid no heed. One of the companions of the Promised Messiah[as] pointed out that Pundit Lekh Rām was offering *salām* to him upon which the Promised Messiah[as] stated, 'He utters filthy words against my master and offers salām to me?' In other words, the envy of the Promised Messiah[as] did not allow him to exchange salutations with one who utters filth against his master.

INTENSITY OF LOVE

It is quite obvious from the writings of the Promised Messiah[as] that there was an ocean of love flowing in his heart for his patron,

Prophet Muḥammad[sa]. His passionate love assumed the shape of a storm, and nothing could stand in the way of its towering and overpowering waves. The following couplets illustrate the intensity of his love:

تا بمن نورِ رسول پاکؐ را بنموده اند
عشقِ او در دل ہمی جوشد جو آب از آبشار
آتش عشق از دمِ من ہمچو برقے می جهد
یک طرف اے ہمدمانِ خادم از گرد و جوار

> Since the time I had seen the light of the Holy Prophet Muḥammad[sa], my love for him has intensified within my heart as the rage of a waterfall. O my friends, move away from me [i.e. take caution] for my burning love for the Holy Prophet[sa] streaks through my breath like lightning.
>
> (*Ā'īna'-e-Kamālāt-e-Islām, Rūḥānī Khazā'in*, vol. 5, p. 27)

TO MOLD ONESELF LIKE THE BELOVED

In perfect love one strives to mould oneself in the manner of the beloved. An attempt is made to imitate the style, demeanour, etiquette and appearance of the beloved. As the degree of love heightens, the attraction towards the qualities of the beloved grows in proportion until at last; it culminates into a mirror image of the beloved. When this takes place no difference remains between the lover and the beloved.

من تو شدم تو من شدی   من تن شدم تو جاں شدی
تاکس نگوید بعد ازیں   من دیگرم تو دیگری

I have become you and you have become me. It is as if I am the body and you are my soul. From this point on no one can say we are two different beings.

Imām Rabbānī *Mujaddid Alf-e-Thānī* has written:

مقتضائے کمال محبت رفعِ اثینیت ست واتحادِ محب محبوب

Meaning, 'Perfect love requires the lover to colour himself in the manner of the beloved. Eventually, the two become one entity.'

(*Maktūbāt-e-Imām Rabbānī*, vol. 3 p. 15, *Maktūb*, no. 88, Maṭba' Nāmī Munshī Naul Kishwar bar Taba' Muzayyan Maqbūl Jahāń Shud)

Ḥaḍrat Sheikh 'Abdul-Qādir Jīlānī writes about himself:

ھذا وجود جدّی محمد صلی اللہ علیہ وسلم لاوجود عبدالقادر

This is not the person of 'Abdul-Qādir, but is of my ancestor, Muḥammad Muṣṭafā, may peace and blessings of Allah be upon him.

(*Tājul-Auliyā',* published in Egypt, p. 35 and *Manāqibi Guldasta-e-Karāmāt*, printed at Iftikhār Press, Delhi)

Muftī Ghulām Sarwar, the writer of the book *Guldasta-e-Karāmāt* (Bouquet of Signs) writes after noting the above quote of Sheikh 'Abdul-Qādir Jīlānī[rh]:

پس یہ کلام معرفت التیام آنحضرتؐ کی دلالت کرتی ہے اوپر فنائے اتم اور محو کامل آنجناب کے بیچ ذات بابرکات آنحضرتؐ کہ از راہِ فرطِ عشق و محبت ذات اور ذات ہو کر فنافی الرسول ہو گئے تھے۔ ذاتاً وصفاتاً، قولاً وفعلاً، حالاً وکمالاً۔

> These words prove that Sheikh 'Abdul-Qādir Jīlānī[rh] had such love for the Holy Prophet[sa] that he moulded himself in his personage and as a result, became just like the Holy Prophet[sa] in person, qualities, words, actions, overall condition and signs.
> (*Guldasta-e-Karāmāt,* printed at Iftikhār-e-Dehli, p. 8)

The Promised Messiah[as], the writer of this Qaṣīdah, also achieved unity with Prophet Muḥammad[sa] through his extreme and perfect love. He writes in his Persian poetry:

محو روئے او شدست ایں روئے من
بوئے او آید زبام و کوئے من
بس کہ من در عشق او ہستم نہاں
من ہمانم، من ہمانم، من ہمان
جان من از جان او یابد غذا
از گریبانم عیان شد آن ذکا

احمد اندر جان احمد شد پدید
اسم من گردید آں اسم وحید

My face has absorbed into his face and you can smell his fragrance from my home and the street whereupon I live. I am lost in his love. In reality I am him, I am him, I am him. My soul is nourished from his soul and the same sun has risen from my person. Aḥmad [i.e. Muḥammad[sa]] has appeared in the body of Aḥmad [i.e. the Promised Messiah[as]] and therefore, I was given the same name which was given to this everlasting human being.

(*Sirāj-e-Munīr, Rūḥānī Khazā'in*, vol. 12, p. 97)

EVERLASTING LIFE

In this state, when a true lover absorbs himself in the love of the beloved, then he discovers that his life is the same as that of his beloved, as quoted in this verse:

ہرگز نمیرد آنکہ دلش زندہ شد بعشق
میرد کسیکہ نیست مرامش مرام شان

(*Satt Bachan, Rūḥānī Khazā'in*, vol. 10, p. 132)

Such a love establishes itself forever and liberates itself from any kind of death. The writer of the Qaṣīdah, the founder of the

Ahmadiyya Muslim Community, maintained this degree of love for the Holy Prophet Muḥammad[sa], which is never ending. He writes:

إِنِّي أَمُوتُ وَلَا يَمُوتُ مَحَبَّتِي

يُدْرَى بِذِكْرِكَ فِي التُّرَابِ نِدَائِي

> Meaning that: O my beloved, even though I will die, my love will live forever and will never die. And when people will be heard from their graves, my voice will be recognized by your praise. Other people will be calling out the names of their loved ones but upon my tongue shall be your name alone. My tongue will be repeating, 'O my beloved Muḥammad[sa], my dear Muḥammad[sa], my adored Muḥammad[sa].'
>
> (*Minanur-Raḥmān, Rūḥānī Khazā'in*, vol. 9, p. 169)

O our Allāh, send Your blessings on Muḥammad[sa] and on his lover the Promised Messiah[as], and shower Your blessings and Your peace.

THE QAṢĪDAH

The following is the first couplet of the Qaṣīdah:

COUPLET 1

يَا عَيْنَ فَيْضِ اللهِ وَ الْعِرْفَانِ
يَسْعٰى إِلَيْكَ الْخَلْقُ كَالظَّمْاٰنِ

O you who are the fountain of Allāh's beneficence and divine understanding;
People throng towards you like the thirsty rushing towards water.

The first couplet of this Qaṣīdah reveals the perfect love of the Promised Messiah[as] for his beloved. Most poets begin their *qaṣīdahs* by describing the physical attributes of their loved ones. They illustrate the prominent qualities or attributes, which remind them of their beloved and the intensity of their love. For example, the first couplet of the Qaṣīdah Mīmiyyah written by Imra'ul-Qais is as follows:

قف بالديار التى لم يعفها القدم

بلى وغيّرها الارواح والديم

O Imra'ul-Qais, pause for a while in these towns where the beloved used to live,
which have not been destroyed, but the winds and rain has changed their condition.

(*Qaṣīdatu Bānat Su'ād li-Ka'b bin Zuhair,* Maqbūl-e-'Ām Press, Lahore, 1941 edition.)

In the same way Ka'b bin Zuhair wrote his Qaṣīdah in praise of the Holy Prophet Muḥammad[sa] which is known by the name Bānat Su'ād. In this Qaṣīdah he first talks about his separation from Su'ād. His physical beauty, his travels and the qualities of his mount are described, subsequent to which he praises the Holy Prophet[sa].

Again 'Allāmah Muḥammad Al-Buṣairī starts his famous Qaṣīdah with the following couplets:

أَمِنْ تَذَكُّرِ جِيْرَانٍ بِذِیْ سَلَمِ

مَزَجْتَ دَمْعًا جَرٰی مِنْ مُقْلَةٍ بِدَمِ

اَمْ هَبَّتِ الرِّيْحُ مِنْ تِلْقَاءِ كَاظِمَةٍ

اَوْ اَوْمَضَ الْبَرْقُ فِي الظَّلْمَاءِ مِنْ اِضَمِ

Are you crying with tears, which have mixed with blood, in the memory of the neighbours of Dhi-Salām (i.e. the people of Medina), or have you been reminded of your beloved by the wind blowing from Medina, or have you seen the lightning in a dark night over the hills of Iḍam (near Medina)?

(*Qaṣīdatul-Burdah li-'Allāmah Al-Buṣairi*, p. 1, Qadīmī Kutub Khānah, Ārām Bāgh, Karachi)

However, the writer of this Qaṣīdah was so absorbed in love, that his beloved was present before him every moment of his life. Accordingly, he directly addresses his beloved with praises, avoiding any surrounding distractions saying:

يَا عَيْنَ فَيْضِ اللّٰهِ وَ الْعِرْفَانِ
يَسْعٰى إِلَيْكَ الْخَلْقُ كَالظَّمْاٰنِ

This couplet of the Qaṣīdah mentions a unique excellence of the Holy Prophet Muḥammad[sa]. In this physical world we see clean and clear water flowing forth from natural springs. In the same manner, the fountainhead and source of all spiritual bounty, blessings and knowledge is the Holy Prophet Muḥammad[sa]. He is the fountain from which all these gifts emanate.

It is an irrefutable fact that when the Holy Prophet Muḥammad[sa] appeared:

دنیا شرک اور بُت پرستی سے بھری ہوئی تھی کوئی پتھر کی پوجا کرتا تھا اور کوئی آگ کی پرستش میں مشغول تھا اور کوئی سورج کے آگے ہاتھ جوڑتا تھا کوئی پانی کو اپنا پرمیشر خیال کرتا تھا اور کوئی انسان کو خدا بنائے بیٹھا تھا علاوہ اسکے زمین ہر قسم کے گناہ اور ظلم اور فساد سے بھری ہوئی تھی جیسا کہ اللہ تعالیٰ نے اس زمانہ کی موجودہ حالت کے

بارہ میں قرآن شریف میں خود گواہی دی ہے اور فرماتا ہے ظَهَرَ الْفَسَادُ فِي الْبَرِّ وَالْبَحْرِ یعنی دریا بھی بگڑ گئے اور خشک زمین بھی بگڑ گئی مطلب یہ کہ جس قوم کے ہاتھ میں کتابِ آسمانی تھی وہ بھی بگڑ گئی اور جن کے ہاتھ میں کتابِ آسمانی نہیں تھی اور خشک جنگل کی طرح تھے وہ بھی بگڑ گئے اور یہ امر ایک ایسا سچّا واقعہ ہے کہ ہر ایک ملک کی تاریخ اس پر گواہ ناطق ہے۔

The entire world was engrossed in paganism and associating partners with God. People worshipped and prayed to lifeless objects like stones, fire and the sun. Some considered water their god while others worshipped human beings.

In addition, the earth was saturated with all kinds of sin, cruelty and mischief. Allāh Himself has expressed the plight of the world at that time in the Holy Qur'ān:

ظَهَرَ الْفَسَادُ فِي الْبَرِّ وَالْبَحْرِ [1]

This means that those nations which were given heavenly books had become misguided, and those who had not received any divine book, and were like a desolate jungle, had also become misguided. So true is this account that every country's history bears witness to it.

(*Chashma-e-Ma'rifat, Rūḥānī Khazā'in*, vol. 23, p. 379)

[1] Corruption has appeared on land and sea. (*ar-Rūm*, 30:42)

A shameful gloom stretched over the corners of the earth, likening it to a dark night. India, which flourished as a religious centre in ancient times, had not only lost its religion, but its basic human values. The Brahmans, hailed as religious leaders, had declared a vast segment of people, reaching in the millions, as untouchables. They were considered eternally unclean, while the Brahmans, who were in power, did as they pleased. Their sin was not considered sin, but was viewed as an act of benevolence.

The religious leaders and temple custodians were worshipped as gods and were indulged in lives of luxury. They incorporated dancing and music as essential parts of worship. Consequently, the temples digressed into centres of wickedness and the general state of religion deteriorated tremendously. At an extreme, the religious values regressed to the point where women worshipped the private parts of men, eventually losing all dignity and status.

The Christian churches in Europe were not any better than the Hindu temples. They were also centres of mischief. In the Holy Qur'ān Allāh has referred to the priests and monks who pledged to relinquish the world for the cause of God as follows:

وَكَثِيرٌ مِّنْهُمْ فٰسِقُونَ

...but many of them are rebellious. (*al-Ḥadīd*, 57:28)

The people that declared themselves the sons and lovers of God became like apes imitating the sinful, and their morality deteriorated in the likeness of swine, shamelessly pursuing their worldly desires.[2] This was the state of religious leaders. As far as the general public was concerned, they worshipped and obeyed those who disobeyed God and trespassed over His boundaries.

Spirituality disappeared altogether. The contemporary religions failed to demonstrate any evidence of a living relationship with God. All fountains of spirituality had dried up. It was under these circumstances that God sent the Holy Prophet Muḥammad[sa] and announced:

.....وَ اَنْزَلْنَا مِنَ السَّمَآءِ مَآءً طَهُوْرًا۔ لِّنُحْیِۦَ بِهٖ بَلْدَةً مَّيْتًا وَّ نُسْقِيَهٗ مِمَّا خَلَقْنَآ اَنْعَامًا وَّ اَنَاسِيَّ كَثِيْرًا۔

We send down pure water from the sky, that We may thereby give life to a dead land, and endow drink to Our creation–cattle and men in great numbers. (*al-Furqān,* 25:49-50)

This means that the spiritually dead nation of Arabia would get life from this water. Then Allāh went on to say that He would provide this water to such nations as are living the life of animals, and in the same manner, He would provide it to those people who were devoid of civilization and culture. This water would bestow upon them the knowledge of God, and create a spiritual revolution in their lives by developing a relationship with their Everlasting God. Thus, by following the Holy Prophet Muḥammad[sa], various people

---

[2] ...of whom He has made apes and swine and *who* worship the Evil One (*al-Mā'idah 5:61*)

from various nations of the world received the spiritual reward of revelation, converse with God, and His blessings.

It has been established that until the Day of Judgement no person after the advent of the Holy Prophet[sa], regardless of religious affiliation, could achieve the status necessary to receive the favours of Allāh until and unless that person followed the path of the Holy Prophet[sa]. By following his footsteps a person was initiated into the community receiving the favours of Allāh. Allāh mentions this blessed group of people in the Holy Qur'ān as follows:

وَ مَنْ يُّطِعِ اللّٰهَ وَ الرَّسُوْلَ فَاُولٰٓئِكَ مَعَ الَّذِيْنَ اَنْعَمَ اللّٰهُ عَلَيْهِمْ مِّنَ النَّبِيّٖنَ وَ
الصِّدِّيْقِيْنَ وَالشُّهَدَآءِ وَالصّٰلِحِيْنَ ۚ وَحَسُنَ اُولٰٓئِكَ رَفِيْقًا ؕ

And whoso obeys Allāh and this Messenger (of His) shall be among those on whom Allāh has bestowed His blessings, namely, the prophets, the truthful, the martyrs, and the righteous. And excellent companions are these. (*an-Nisā'*, 4:70)

In other words, the spiritual blessings of Allāh will be showered exclusively on those who obey Allāh and the Holy Prophet[sa]. The four degrees of spirituality mentioned in the verse (i.e. prophethood, truthfulness, martyrdom, and righteousness) can be attained solely by those completely submitting to Allāh and the Holy Prophet[sa].

The perfect knowledge by which all doubts and ambiguities are removed, and by which nearness to Allāh is achieved resulting in direct communication with Him, can only be acquired by the followers of the Holy Prophet[sa]. All other people belonging to other faiths, be they Hindus or Jews, Zoroastrians or Buddhists, Christians or followers of any other religion, will be deprived of this grand favour of Allāh. It is a fact that the door of direct communication with Allāh has been closed to all religions except Islam. It should be understood that their deprivation is a result of their own actions, which led them astray from the right path.

Innately within every human being is a great and powerful urge to speak to, listen to and see the one they love most. This develops an understanding of the beloved. Similarly, a comprehensive understanding of Allāh cannot be achieved unless one can hear His eloquent and harmonious voice. True lovers of Allāh prostrate their heads on the ground crying and supplicating in extreme humility for Him to respond. They could never be satisfied with His silence. True love cannot tolerate such an offense. Human nature demands to hear the satisfying sound of the beloved. Persistent thoughts arise from within the depths of the heart to quench this desire as it is written:

عشق می خواہد کلامِ یار را
رو بپرس از عاشق ایں اسرار را

Love demands the beloved to converse with the lover.
Inquire from the one who knows the secrets of this love.

(*Barāhīn-e-Aḥmadiyya*, Part 3, Footnote 11,
Rūḥānī Khazā'in, vol. 1, p. 172)

Since the Holy Prophet[sa] is unrivalled in his love for Allāh and he maintains the knowledge of the secrets of this love, he has no match in introducing the searchers to Allāh the Almighty. This being the case, Allāh has responded to the natural requests of His lovers in the following words:

إِنْ كُنْتُمْ تُحِبُّوْنَ اللّٰهَ فَاتَّبِعُوْنِيْ يُحْبِبْكُمُ اللّٰهُ

If you love Allāh, follow me, then Allāh will love you and forgive you your faults.' And Allāh is Most Forgiving, Merciful. (*Āl-e-'Imrān*, 3:32)

This verse addresses such people who claim to love Allāh. If they are truthful in their claim and sincerely desire to meet their Lord, then they should follow the Holy Prophet[sa]. He will take them to Allāh and the result of this nearness and union will be Allāh's reciprocated love.

At another place Allāh says:

وَإِذَا سَأَلَكَ عِبَادِيْ عَنِّيْ فَإِنِّيْ قَرِيْبٌ ۖ أُجِيْبُ دَعْوَةَ الدَّاعِ إِذَا دَعَانِ

And when My servants ask you about Me (say): 'I am near. I answer the prayer of the supplicant when he prays to Me'. (*al-Baqarah*, 2:187)

The above verses make it obvious that the only door open to Allāh is through the Holy Prophet[sa]. All other spiritual fountains have dried. However, one spring is still flourishing and will never suffer depletion. It is the fountain of the Holy Prophet[sa]. There exists no other method or means of achieving spiritual heights and blessings from Allāh. The Promised Messiah[as], the writer of this Qaṣīdah, had emphasized this important point by stating it in the very first of seventy couplets praising his beloved Muḥammad[sa].

Therefore, the Holy Prophet[sa] is the fountainhead of all spiritual bounty, blessings and knowledge of Allāh. People thirsting for the love of Allāh and eagerly searching to find Him, pursue the Holy Prophet[sa], in order to quench their thirst from this blessed and bountiful fountain.

COUPLET 2

يَا بَحْرَ فَضْلِ الْمُنْعِمِ الْمَنَّانِ
تَهْوِىْ إِلَيْكَ الزُّمَرُ بِالْكِيْزَانِ

O you who are the ocean of the Grace of the Benefactor and Bountiful God;
People flock to you with empty cups in their hands.

In the first couplet the Holy Prophet[sa] was described as a fountain. However, a fountain can be limited to a small area, restricting its advantages to a few people. The second couplet describes the universality of the Holy Prophet's[sa] message by likening him to an ocean. This metaphorically depicts the blessings from the Holy Prophet[sa] as vast as the width and depth of an ocean, as opposed to the limitations of a fountain. People can benefit from the Holy Prophet[sa] in great multitudes as they would from an ocean.

COUPLET 3

يَا شَمْسَ مُلْكِ الْحُسْنِ وَالْإِحْسَانِ
نَوَّرْتَ وَجْهَ الْبَرِّ وَ الْعُمْرَانِ

O you the sun of the kingdom of beauty and virtue;
You have illuminated the deserts as well as the cities.

In this couplet the blessings of the Holy Prophet[sa] are likened to the sun. The sun indiscriminately showers its rays of light upon both, the uninhabited areas such as the jungles and deserts, and the densely populated cities and villages, except upon those who put a curtain between themselves and the sun. In the same manner the Holy Prophet[sa] is the sun of spiritual knowledge and his light is a blessing for people of all religions, excluding those who isolate themselves from this sun, or are blind in their hearts. The Holy Qur'ān states that whom Allāh gives no light, for him there is no light at all. (*an-Nūr*, 24:41)

At another place the Promised Messiah[as] describes the beauty and benevolence of the Holy Prophet[sa] in the following Persian couplet:

صد هزاران یوسفے بینم درین چاه ذقن
وآن مسیح ناصری شد از دم او بے شمار

> The beauty in the dimple of the Holy Prophet's[sa] chin is equivalent to hundreds of thousands of Yūsufs [Josephs].
>
> (*Ā'īna'-e-Kamālāt-e-Islām, Rūḥānī Khazā'in*, vol. 5, p. 27)

One meaning of this couplet is that the beauty of the Holy Prophet[sa] exceeds that of thousands of Josephs. Another meaning is that a thousand Josephs, in spite of their own exceptional beauty, are enchanted by the beauty of the Holy Prophet[sa].

The spiritual status of the Holy Prophet[sa] is so highly exalted that by the blessings of his spirit countless number of Messiahs like the Messiah of Nazareth, have already appeared amongst his followers. Many more are yet to appear. The Promised Messiah[as] writes about the true followers of the Holy Prophet[sa]:

> وہی شربت نہایت کثرت سے نہایت لطافت سے نہایت لذت سے پیتے ہیں اور پی رہے ہیں۔ اسرائیلی نور ان میں روشن ہیں۔ بنی یعقوب کے پیغمبروں کی ان میں برکتیں ہیں۔ سبحان اللہ ثم سبحان اللہ حضرت خاتم الانبیاء صلی اللہ علیہ وسلم کس شان کے نبی ہیں۔ اللہ اللہ کیا عظیم الشان نور ہے جس کے ناچیز خادم جس کی ادنی سے ادنی امت۔ جس کے احقر سے احقر چاکر مراتب مذکورہ بالا تک پہنچ جاتے ہیں۔

> The same drink, which was given to Moses, Jesus and other prophets, has been enjoyed by numerous followers of the Holy Prophet[sa] in elegance and abundance. Some are even enjoying it today. The light of the Israelite prophets burns bright within them. They have attained the same blessings that were given to the Children of Jacob. Holy is Allāh, then again, Holy is Allāh! How eminent a status is that of the Holy Prophet[sa] and how great is

that light! People who are his servants, his lowly followers, can achieve the high status just mentioned.

(*Barāhīn-e-Aḥmadiyya*, Part 3, *Rūḥānī Khazā'in*, vol. 1, p. 272, footnote no.11)

As Jesus of Nazareth used to give life to the spiritually dead, the followers of the Holy Prophet[sa] breathe life into lifeless hearts and serve drinks rendering spiritual life. For example, Sheikh Mu'īn-ud-Dīn Ajmerī[rh] has dubbed himself the second Jesus in one of his Persian couplets:

دمبدم روح القدس اندر معینے مے دمد
من نمے گوئم مگر من عیسیٰؑ ثانی شدم

My beloved blows the Holy Spirit into me every moment of my life,
And I cannot say anything but that I have become the second Jesus.

(*Kulliyāt-e-Mathnawī,* Maulānā Jalāl-ud-Dīn Rūmī, vol.4, p. 29, Qaṣīdah Mithl-e-Qāni' Shudan Ādmi, Printed by Intishārāt Kitābchai, Tehran)

In addition, Maulānā Jalāl-ud-Dīn Rūmī has stated in one of his poems that:

عیسیم لیکن ہر آن کو یافت جان   از دمِ من او بماند جاودان
شد ز عیسیٰ زندہ لیکن باز مُرد   شاد آن کو جان بدین عیسیٰ سپرد

> He is Jesus. The dead who were given life by Jesus died spiritually again, but to rejoice because those who devoted themselves to this Jesus (i.e. Maulānā Rūmī) would live forever.
>
> (*Kulliyāt-e-Mathnawī,* Maulānā Jalāl-ud-Dīn Rūmī, vol. 4, p. 29, Qaṣīdah Mithl-e-Qāni' Shudan Ādmi, Printed by Intishārāt Kitābchai, Tehran)

As the writer of this Qaṣīdah considered the Holy Prophet[sa] to be the sun of beauty and benevolence, nothing in the world could restrain his love for him, nor could anyone interfere in this relationship. At another place he writes in Persian:

بسے سہل است از دنیا بریدن بیادِ حسن و احسانِ محمدؐ

بدیگر دلبرے کارے ندارم کہ ہستم کشتۂ آنِ محمدؐ

> When I ponder over the beauty and benevolence of the Holy Prophet[sa], it is effortless for me to forget the entire world, and I have nothing to do with any other because I am dissolved in the glory of Muḥammad[sa].
>
> (*Ā'īna'-e-Kamālāt-e-Islām, Rūḥānī Khazā'in,* vol. 5, p. 649)

COUPLET 4

قَوْمٌ رَّأَوْكَ وَ اُمَّـةٌ قَدْ اُخْبِرَتْ
مِنْ ذٰلِكَ الْبَدْرِ الَّذِیْ أَصْبَانِیْ

A nation was blessed by having been able to see you,
While many heard of the full moon which has captivated my heart.

The question arises here that if the Holy Prophet[sa] is the sun of the spiritual world, then why were nations before and after his advent deprived of his light. The answer to this question is presented in this couplet by describing that the blessings of the Holy Prophet[sa] are for all ages. They were prevalent in the past in the sense that the prophets of past nations prophesied about his advent as Allāh advised them. For example, we find that Moses prophesied in Deuteronomy 18:18 that Allāh would raise a prophet from among the Ishmaelites who were the brethren of the Israelites like unto them. The prophecy stated that Allāh would converse with him.

Ḥaḍrat Moses was also told about the majestic station of the Holy Prophet[sa] and that the final and complete *shariah* [law] would be given to him. In response to this Ḥaḍrat Moses desired to see this great miracle of Allāh and he requested Allāh رَبِّ اَرِنِیْٓ اَنْظُرْ اِلَیْکَ (*al-A'rāf*, 7:144) meaning, O my lord! Show me the same manifestation that will be shown to the Holy Prophet[sa]. Allāh responded by stating that Moses[as] could not bear this manifestation. The manifestation in question was reserved for the Holy Prophet[sa]. However, Allāh said that He would reveal this manifestation upon a mountain. If the mountain could withstand it, then Moses[as] would be able to experience it. فَلَمَّا تَجَلّٰى رَبُّهٗ لِلْجَبَلِ (*al-A'rāf*, 7:144).

When the manifestation unveiled itself upon the mountain, جَعَلَهٗ دَكًّا وَّ خَرَّ مُوْسٰى صَعِقًا there was an earthquake that shattered the mountain into pieces. Ḥaḍrat Moses[as] fainted. When he regained consciousness, he praised Allāh and asked for forgiveness and said: وَ اَنَا اَوَّلُ الْمُؤْمِنِيْنَ

I am the first to believe in the Prophet who is to receive this manifestation.

In the Holy Qur'ān, Allāh Himself has referred to this acceptance by Ḥaḍrat Moses:

شَهِدَ شَاهِدٌ مِّنْ بَنِيْٓ اِسْرَآءِيْلَ عَلٰى مِثْلِهٖ فَاٰمَنَ وَاسْتَكْبَرْتُمْ

Say, 'Tell me, if this is from Allāh and you disbelieve therein, and a witness from among the Children of Israel bears witness to (the advent of) one like him, and he believed, but you are too proud, (how should you fare?)' Verily, Allāh guides not the wrongdoing people. (*al-Aḥqāf*, 46:11)

This very point has been made by Imām Sharf-ud-Dīn Abū 'Abdullāh Muḥammad bin Sa'īd al-Buṣairī[rh] who writes in his Qaṣīdah:

مَا مَضَتْ فَتْرَةٌ مِّنَ الرُّسُلِ إِلَّا

بَشَّرَتْ قَوْمَهَا بِكَ الْأَنْبِيَاءُ

There is no age in which a prophet appeared,
And did not prophesy about your advent (i.e. the Holy Prophet[sa]).

(*Dīwānul-Buṣairī*, p. 2, Maṭbū'ah Muṣṭafā Al-Bābī Al-Ḥalabī, 1955)

Furthermore, the couplet refers to the Qur'ānic prophecy of a future advent of the reflection of the Holy Prophet[sa] in the latter days. This is mentioned in the chapter al-Jumu'ah as follows.

وَّآخَرِيْنَ مِنْهُمْ لَمَّا يَلْحَقُوْا بِهِمْ ۚ وَهُوَ الْعَزِيْزُ الْحَكِيْمُ

...and (among) others from among them who have not yet joined them. He is the Mighty, the Wise. (*al-Jumu'ah*, 62:4)

The couplet alludes to this second advent, which was to reflect the light of the Holy Prophet[sa]. This is why the Holy Prophet[sa] is referred to as the full moon. The moon has no light of its own, but simply reflects the light of the sun. As described in couplet three, The Holy Prophet's[sa] first advent resembled the sun, radiating powerful and commanding light. During this dispensation the Holy Prophet's[sa] majestic qualities dominated. These qualities are related to his majestic name *Muḥammad*. However, his second advent would emphasize the beauty, compassion and elegance of Islam through a reformer who would appear in his image. This is the reason that this couplet illustrates the Holy Prophet[sa] as the full moon, reflecting the light of the sun to people in a time of darkness.

COUPLETS 5 and 6

يَبْكُوْنَ مِنْ ذِكْرِ الْجَمَالِ صَبَابَةً
وَ تَأَلُّمًا مِّنْ لَّوْعَةِ الْهِجْرَانِ

People shed tears when they fondly reminisce of your grace and beauty;
A fire consumes their hearts due to the pains of separation.

وَ أَرَى الْقُلُوْبَ لَدَى الْحَنَاجِرِ كُرْبَةً
وَ أَرَى الْغُرُوْبَ تُسِيْلُهَا الْعَيْنَانِ

I see their hearts are in such anxiety as if they have reached their throats;
I see that their eyes are flowing with tears.

When one is deeply in love with another, separation from the beloved is very painful for the lover. At times the sorrow of separation brings forth tears from the eyes. Allāmah Buṣairī[rh] writes in his Qaṣīdah referring to the same condition:

أَمِنْ تَذَكُّرِ جِيْرَانٍ بِذِیْ سَلَمٍ

مَزَجْتَ دَمْعًا جَرٰی مِنْ مُقْلَةٍ بِدَمٍ

Are you profusely crying in the memory of the neighbours of Dhi-Salām i.e. Prophet Muḥammad[sa] and the people of Medina,
That tears are flowing from your eyes have mixed in blood?

(*Qaṣīdatul-Burdah li-'Allāmah Al-Buṣairi*, p. 1, Qadīmī Kutub Khānah, Ārām Bāgh, Karachi)

This refers to excessive crying. A smaller element always mixes into a larger one. For example, we mix salt into flour. In the same manner, mixing tears into blood points to excessive crying which has exhausted the tears, and if there are a few left, they have mixed into blood. The remaining substance flowing from the eyes is nothing other than blood. If the tears comprise any part of it, they are insignificant as salt is in dough.

COUPLET 7

يَا مَنْ غَدَا فِیْ نُوْرِهٖ وَ ضِيَائِهٖ

كَالنَّيِّرَيْنِ وَ نُوْرَ الْمَلَوَانِ

O you who are the sun and moon of light;
You have illuminated the day and the night.

In a verse of the Holy Qur'ān, the Arabic word *ḍiyā'* has been used as the sun and the word *nūr* has been used for the moon as follows:

هُوَ الَّذِىْ جَعَلَ الشَّمْسَ ضِيَآءً وَّالْقَمَرَ نُوْرًا . . .

He it is Who has made the sun radiant (ḍiyā' - a brilliant light) and the moon lambent (nūr—a lustrous reflector)... (*Yūnus*, 10:6)

The word *ḍiyā'* means direct light from its source and *nūr* only means a reflection. The Promised Messiah[as] has used this point in the couplet under discussion to describe the spiritual perfection of the Holy Prophet[sa] as the sun and moon.

As in the physical world the sun is the central point, the Holy Prophet[sa] is the central point in the spiritual world. Being the sun of the spiritual world, only his light can extinguish the world's darkness. In his absence, spiritual darkness would be confronted by other persons who would function like the moon and stars in his service. Allāh says in the Holy Qur'ān:

تَبٰرَكَ الَّذِىْ جَعَلَ فِى السَّمَآءِ بُرُوْجًا وَّجَعَلَ فِيْهَا سِرٰجًا وَّقَمَرًا مُّنِيْرًا

Blessed is He Who has made constellations [of stars] in the heaven and has placed therein a Lamp (the sun) and Moon – both luminous. (*al-Furqān*, 25:62)

Building upon the above analogy, we find twelve constellations of stars in the physical world as we know it. These have been named Aries, Taurus, Gemini, Cancer, Leo, Virgo, Libra, Scorpio,

Sagittarius, Capricorn, Aquarius and Pisces. Allāh has also created twelve constellations in the spiritual world.

In the Holy Qur'ān (*Nūḥ*, 71:17) the sun has been described as a lamp. It says:

وَّجَعَلَ الشَّمْسَ سِرَاجًا

In Sūrah an-Nabā' the sun has been described as وَهَّاج which means that it is the source of light and its heat can be felt at long distances. Similarly, the Holy Qur'ān describes the Holy Prophet[sa] in the following verse likening him to the sun, by referring to him as a light giving lamp:

يٰۤاَيُّهَا النَّبِيُّ اِنَّاۤ اَرْسَلْنٰكَ شَاهِدًا وَّمُبَشِّرًا وَّنَذِيْرًا ﴿۳۵﴾
وَّدَاعِيًا اِلَى اللّٰهِ بِاِذْنِهٖ وَسِرَاجًا مُّنِيْرًا ﴿۳۶﴾

> **O Prophet, truly We have sent thee as a witness, and a bearer of glad tidings, and a warner, and as a summoner unto Allāh by His command, and as a radiant lamp (that gives bright light.)** (*al-Aḥzāb*, 33:46–47)

We find in the books of *Aḥādīth* that Allāh will raise at the head of every century a reformer who would revive the religion of Islam.[3] We also find indications in the *Aḥādīth* of the coming of the Messiah and Mahdi at the head of the fourteenth Islamic century.

---

[3] *Sunan Abī Dāwūd, Kitābul-Malāḥim*, Bābu Mā Yudhkaru Fī Qarnil-Mi'atī, Ḥadīth no. 4291

If we disregard the first century in which the Holy Prophet[sa] appeared, and the fourteenth century in which the Promised Messiah[as] appeared, we are left with twelve centuries, each in which at least one reformer was to appear. These twelve reformers are the twelve constellations of stars in the spiritual universe. The reformers would obtain their light from the Holy Prophet[sa] in the same way the moon derives its light from the sun. Their light would not be their own, but simply a reflection of the light of the Holy Prophet[sa]. The Promised Messiah[as], the *Mujaddid* [Reformer] of the fourteenth century, has stated in his Persian poetry:

این آتشم ز آتش مہر محمدؐ یست
و این آبِ من ز آبِ زلالِ محمدؐ است

The fire of love that I possess I have received directly through the love of Muḥammad[sa],
And the soul purifying water that I possess is from the fountain of Muḥammad[sa].

(*Ā'īna'-e-Kamālāt-e-Islām, Rūḥānī Khazā'in*, vol. 5, p. 645)

He also states in his book *Ḥaqīqatul-Waḥī*:

وہی ہے جو سرچشمہ ہر ایک فیض کا ہے اور وہ شخص جو بغیر اقرار افاضہ اُس کے کسی فضیلت کا دعویٰ کرتا ہے۔ وہ انسان نہیں ہے بلکہ ذُرّیّتِ شیطان ہے کیونکہ ہر ایک فضیلت کی کُنجی اُسکو دی گئی ہے اور ہر ایک معرفت کا خزانہ اُسکو عطا کیا گیا ہے۔ جو اُسکے ذریعہ سے نہیں پاتا وہ محروم ازلی ہے----اس آفتاب ہدایت کی شعاع دُھوپ کی

طرح ہم پر پڑتی ہے اور اُسی وقت تک ہم مُنور رہ سکتے ہیں جبتک کہ ہم اُس کے مقابل
پر کھڑے ہیں۔

He [Muḥammad[sa]] is the fountain of all knowledge and beneficence, and if anyone self proclaims any excellence outside of the Holy Prophet[sa], then such a person is not human, rather, the child of Satan. The key to every excellence and the treasure of all spiritual knowledge has been given to him. If a person fails to acquire anything from him, such a person will be a loser for eternity... The [spiritual] light of the guiding sun shines upon us just like the sunlight, and we can only shine while we are standing in its presence.

(*Ḥaqīqatul-Waḥī, Rūḥānī Khazā'in*, vol. 22, p. 119)

Whether it is day or night, everything receives its light from the Holy Prophet[sa].

COUPLETS 8 and 9

يَا بَدْرَنَا يَا اٰيَةَ الرَّحْمٰنِ
أَهْدَى الْهُدَاةِ وَ أَشْجَعَ الشُّجْعَانِ

O our full moon and sign of the Gracious God;
O the best of all guides, the bravest of the brave.

إِنِّىْ أَرٰى فِىْ وَجْهِكَ الْمُتَهَلِّلِ
شَأْنًا يَّفُوْقُ شَمَائِلَ الْاِنْسَانِ

I find such a glory in your sparkling countenance;
That surpasses all human excellence.

In this couplet the Holy Prophet[sa] has been addressed as the full moon in relation to his ability to guide humanity. The quality of light that Allāh granted him was not given to any other. That sublime light was not bestowed upon the angels or the stars, or upon the moon or the sun. Rubies, emeralds, sapphires and pearls all failed at the same. In short, it was not given to anything else, be it on the earth or in the heavens above. He reflected the Light of Allāh in perfection, and therefore, he was to Allāh as the moon was to the sun.

The Holy Prophet[sa] was also the reflection of Allāh's quality *ar-Raḥmān* (الرحمن : The Gracious). Being the Gracious, Allāh bestows blessings upon His creation indiscriminately. He has provided in the physical world the sun, moon, air, water, etc. without which human life cannot exist. In the same manner He revealed the Holy Qur'ān to the Holy Prophet[sa] upon which all spiritual life is dependant. Then the Holy Prophet[sa] proceeded to deliver the Message to the people with the spirit inherent within his nature. Allāh says in the Holy Qur'ān:

قُلْ مَآ اَسْـَٔلُكُمْ عَلَيْهِ مِنْ اَجْرٍ وَّمَآ اَنَا مِنَ الْمُتَكَلِّفِيْنَ ﴿٨٧﴾

Say, 'I ask not of you any reward for it, nor am I of those who are given to affectation'. (*Ṣād*, 38:87)

This couplet also addresses the Holy Prophet[sa] as the greatest of guides. Of all guides who have appeared in this world, the most exalted is the group who achieved the rank of prophets. All Prophets who preceded the Holy Prophet[sa] from time to time, were sent to particular nations at particular times. However, the Holy Prophet[sa] was sent to all nations and all ethnicities. This is why the Holy Prophet[sa] stands alone explicitly declaring to humankind that he was the prophet of Allāh sent to all.

قُلْ يٰٓاَيُّهَا النَّاسُ اِنِّيْ رَسُوْلُ اللّٰهِ اِلَيْكُمْ جَمِيْعًا

Say, 'O Mankind! Truly I am a Messenger to you all from Allāh'... (*al-A'rāf*, 7:159)

This declaration meant that he would have to challenge all religions and nations. The other prophets could not make this statement because they were not endowed with the perfection or power required for the reformation of the world. This commanding rank of glory and grandeur was not given to anyone but to the Holy Prophet[sa].

No other prophet achieved the level of success accomplished by the Holy Prophet[sa]. The Promised Messiah[as] wrote with relation to the era of his beloved, the Holy Prophet[sa] as follows:

> It was a jungle into which the Holy Prophet[sa] stepped, where darkness raged rampant. It is my religion [to believe] that if the Holy Prophet[sa] was not involved, and all of the prophets who had gone before him were brought together and desired to achieve the same work and reformation that the Holy Prophet[sa] had

accomplished, they would not be able to do so. They were not given the heart or the strength to. Should someone say, 'Allāh pardon, this is an insult to the other prophets,' then that foolish person falsely accuses me. I consider it part of my faith to respect and revere all of the prophets. However, the superiority of the Holy Prophet[sa] over the other prophets is an even greater part of my faith, and is integral to my being. It is not within my control to remove this thought. An unfortunate and blind opponent may say whatever he wishes, but I [persist to] claim that the achievements of the Holy Prophet[sa] could not have been accomplished by any other individual, nor any group put together. This is merely the blessing of Allāh, and He bestows His blessings upon whomsoever He wills.

(*Malfūẓāt*, vol. 1, p. 420, printed in India, 2003 edition.)

THE BRAVEST PERSON

Every hour of the twenty-three years the Holy Prophet[sa] lived after his claim to prophethood stands proof of his unparalleled bravery. I shall mention only one incident of his bravery here. In the Battle of Ḥunain, the Muslim army, which consisted of 12,000 soldiers, started retreating from the battlefront and the Holy Prophet[sa] was left with only 12 people. The enemy was launching wave after wave of arrows. At this point, Ḥaḍrat Abū Bakr[ra] descended from his mount and took hold of the reigns of the mule that the Holy Prophet[sa] was riding and said: 'O Prophet of Allāh! Why don't you retreat a little until the Muslim army regroups?'

The Holy Prophet[sa] replied: 'Abū Bakr, release the reigns of my mule!'

Then the Holy Prophet[sa] spurred his mule forward into the narrow pass along which the enemy was shooting arrows from both sides. In this fearful and formidable situation the Holy Prophet[sa] was reciting a couplet:

انا النبی لا کذب

انا ابن عبد المطلب

I am the prophet, not a liar!
I am the son of 'Abdul-Muṭṭalib.
(*Ṣaḥīḥul-Bukhārī,* Kitābul-Jihādi Was-Siyar, Bābu Man Qāda Dābbata Ghairihī Fil-Ḥarb, Ḥadīth no. 2864)

In such a predicament, when the enemy is gaining ground and their victory is apparent, even the bravest of the brave lose their senses in desperation. It is not that they fear death, but that they have a greater fear of imprisonment. They dread submitting to the enemy, and seek all avenues of refuge from the battlefield. They would much rather prefer death before surrendering to their foes.

In World War II, when the Russians invaded Berlin, Adolf Hitler committed suicide. Similarly, Ali Muḥammad Bāb, who claimed to be better than the Holy Prophet[sa], discovered that he was going to be killed. He told his friends that my enemies will kill me tomorrow degradingly. Therefore, one of you should kill me because I prefer to be killed by a friend over foe.

On the other hand, the Holy Prophet[sa] not only refrained from wanting to leave the battlefield, but continued advancing and was reciting couplets to arouse the emotion of his soldiers. Apparently, he wanted to communicate to his enemies that they should not mistake the Muslim army's retreat as proof that he was not a prophet. He was adamantly declaring that he was a prophet and would undoubtedly prevail. Although, the retreat of the Muslim army was a temporary setback, the final victory would be his.

The enemy might have viewed the Prophet's determined bravery and solitary advance upon their large attacking army, while proceeding unharmed, as a supernatural event. In order to ensure the enemy did not mistake him for God he was reciting, 'I am a human being and the son [i.e. grandson] of 'Abdul-Muṭṭalib.'

The recorded statements of the Holy Prophet's[sa] companions paint the Holy Prophet[sa] as the bravest among them.[4] Therefore, the quality of the Holy Prophet[sa] mentioned in this couplet has been substantiated with historical facts.

COUPLET 10

وَ قَدِ اقْتَفَاكَ أُولُو النُّهٰى وَبِصِدْقِهِمْ
وَ دَعُوْا تَذَكُّرَ مَعْهَدِ الْاَوْطَانِ

The wise chose your company and followed you;
And the truthful relinquished their hearths and homes to be with you.

Jesus Christ is reported to have said that a tree is recognized by its fruit (Matthew 12:33). Therefore, the writer of this Qaṣīdah

[4] *Ṣaḥīḥ Muslim,* Kitābul-Faḍā'il, Bābu Fi Shajā'atin-Nabiyyi Wa Taqaddumihī Lil-Ḥarb, Ḥadīth no. 5900

initially mentioned the personal qualities and excellences of the Holy Prophet[sa] throughout the first nine couplets. The Promised Messiah[as] now presents the example of the Holy Prophet's followers as proof of the Holy Prophet's truth and eminence. This subject is covered from verses 10 through 19.

William Muir, a prejudiced enemy of Islam, has admitted that Abū Bakr[ra] was very wise, farsighted and highly revered. Similarly, many other companions were renowned for their intelligence and integrity among their families and communities.

(*Life of Mahomet,* by Sir William Muir, p. 62, printed in London 1878)

When considering the manner in which the companions of the Holy Prophet[sa] obeyed him, it is impossible to find a parallel among the earlier prophets. Moses[as] led the Children of Israel to freedom from the Pharaoh. In accordance with the promise of Allāh, he ordered them to enter the Promised Land. Not only did they refuse to act upon this command, but they rudely replied to him, 'You and your God go and fight with the enemy and we will remain here.' (*al-Mā'idah*)

On the other hand, we have the example of the Holy Prophet[sa] at the time of the Battle of Badr. The Muslims of Medina, the *Anṣār*, had pledged to protect the Muslims of Mecca, the emigrants, within the boundaries of Medina. Keeping this agreement in mind, the Holy Prophet[sa] asked the *Anṣār* if they would be willing to fight outside the limits of Medina. The *Anṣār* answered, 'O Prophet of Allāh, we will not act like the companions of Moses [saying] that you and your God should fight the enemy and we shall stay behind. We will fight on your right and on your left, in front of you and behind you. The opponent will not be able to reach you until and unless he walks over our dead bodies. O Prophet of Allāh, if you order us to run our horses into the ocean, we will take our horses and run into the ocean without delay.' (*As-Sīratun-Nabawiyyah,* Ibni Hishām, Dhikru Ru'yā 'Ātikata binti 'Abdil-Muṭṭalib..., p. 420–421, Dārul-Kutubil-'Ilmiyyah, Beirut, 2001)

The companions of the Holy Prophet[sa] followed him as their beloved, and they considered it a blessing for themselves in this world as well as the next, to fulfil his commands. Once the Holy Prophet[sa] was delivering a sermon at *Masjid-e-Nabawī* [i.e. the Prophet's Mosque]. Ḥaḍrat 'Abdullāh bin Rawāḥah[ra] of the *Khazraj* tribe, was a notable poet and was respected as a very devout Muslim. He was passing by on a nearby street when he heard the voice of the Holy Prophet[sa], *"Sit down."* He immediately sat down and remained sitting until the completion of the sermon. (*Kanzul-'Ummāl Fī Sunanil-Aqwāli Wal-Af'āl,* Kitābul-Faḍā'ili, Faḍā'iliṣ-Ṣaḥābah, vol. 13, p. 194, Ḥarfil-'Ain, Dhikru 'Abdillāh bin Rawāḥah, Ḥadīth no. 37, 167, Dārul-Kutubil-'Ilmiyyah, Beirut, 2001)

It is likely that a worldly person who has forsaken God would object to this kind of reaction. It is hard to understand the magnitude of faith and devotion that burned within the hearts of the companions of the Holy Prophet[sa]. The sentiment behind the action of 'Abdullāh bin Rawāḥah[ra] was that it was his duty to immediately act upon any command from the Holy Prophet[sa] which reached his ears. He feared that if he did not obey the command, he might be counted amongst those who rejected the command of the Prophet.

In essence, the companions of the Holy Prophet[sa] followed him with the utmost sincerity, determination, love and devotion. They left their hometowns, places of birth and residences in such a manner as to completely forget about them. Even when Mecca was conquered and the sounds of God's greatness echoed from the deserts, hills, mountains, valleys, cities and villages of Arabia, the emigrants decided to return and remain in Medina with the Holy Prophet[sa].

This couplet also brought about a great change in me. We used to study in the Aḥmadiyya School in Qadian (India). We were off on Fridays and we would return to our hometown, Sekhwāń. It is about three miles from Qadian. Once the principal of the school, Sheikh 'Abdur-Raḥmān Ṣāḥib Miṣrī, came to our village and commented to my late father, Imām-ud-Dīn, how people go to Qadian on Fridays for the congregational prayers, but we children go back to our villages. He disapproved of our actions. However, we students had great love for our village, which was the place of our birth and residence. Therefore, Sheikh Ṣāḥib's advice had no impact on us.

In 1917 or 1918, I accompanied Ḥāfiẓ Roshan 'Alī[ra], a companion of the Promised Messiah[as], to Lahore to attend a convention. At that time the Ahmadis of Lahore prayed at the house of Ḥaḍrat Miāń Chirāgh Dīn outside the Delhi Gate. One day after the *maghrib* prayer [evening prayer], the late Ḥaḍrat Ḥāfiẓ Ṣāḥib recited a few couplets of this Qaṣīdah in a very melodious voice. When he recited this couplet it touched my heart so deeply that the love for my village disappeared. Following this event I rarely visited my village, and eventually stopped completely. Later on, my late father left the village and moved to Qadian as his place of residence.

COUPLET 11

قَدْ اٰثَرُوْكَ وَ فَارَقُوْا أَحْبَابَهُمْ
وَ تَبَاعَدُوْا مِنْ حَلْقَةِ الْاِخْوَانِ

They chose you, and abandoned their friends;
They distanced themselves from their families.

History bears witness that the people who accepted the Holy Prophet[sa] abandoned their towns, homes, and even their relatives for the sake of the Holy Prophet[sa]. They gave precedence to him over all others in every manner and circumstance. So established was this fact that God testified to this very fact Himself, in the Holy Qur'ān where He says:

لَا تَجِدُ قَوْمًا يُّؤْمِنُوْنَ بِاللّٰهِ وَ الْيَوْمِ الْاٰخِرِ يُوَآدُّوْنَ مَنْ حَآدَّ اللّٰهَ وَ رَسُوْلَهٗ وَ لَوْ كَانُوْٓا
اٰبَآءَهُمْ اَوْ اَبْنَآءَهُمْ اَوْ اِخْوَانَهُمْ اَوْ عَشِيْرَتَهُمْ

You will not find any people who believe in Allāh and the Last Day loving those who oppose Allāh and His messenger, even though they be their fathers or their sons or their brethren or their kindred... (*al-Mujādalah*, 58:23)

I recall two incidents from Islamic history illustrating this fact. First, Ḥaḍrat 'Abdur-Raḥmān, the son of Ḥaḍrat Abū Bakr[ra], did not accept Islam until after the Battle of Uḥud. After becoming a Muslim, he once said to his father, 'At one point during the battle you were within my range but I did not strike you because you were my father.'

Ḥaḍrat Abū Bakr[ra] immediately replied, 'By God, if you were in my range I would have certainly killed you and would not have cared the least because you had come there to fight against the Prophet of Allāh.' (*Ar-Rauḍul-Unuf,* Imām Suhailī, vol.3, p. 89–90, Couplet of Ḥassān, Dārul-Kutubil-'Ilmiyyah, Beirut, 2004)

The second incident involves Ḥaḍrat Sa'd bin Abī Waqqāṣ[ra]. He used to take care of his mother and was very charitable towards her. She was adamantly opposed to his acceptance of Islam. When she realized her advice and efforts were unsuccessful, and noticed that Sa'd had no intention of leaving his Faith, she became desperate. She said that she would give up eating and would not resume until he gave up Islam, and if he did not then she would die of hunger and the people would consider him the murderer of his mother. He put forth his best effort to get her to eat, but she would not. On the third day he said to her:

وَاللهِ لَوْ كَانَتْ لَكِ مائةُ نَفْسٍ فَخَرَجَتْ نفَساً نفساً مَا تَرَكْتُ دِيْنِي هٰذا الشَيْئٍ

Meaning, 'I swear in the name of Allāh, that if you possessed not one life, but one hundred lives, and they were to die one at a time, even then I would not give up my religion. It is up to you whether you chose to eat or not.'

(*Tafsīrul-Qur'ānil-'Aẓīm,* Ibni Kathir, vol. 6, p. 301, Tafsīru Sūrati Luqmān, under verse no. 16, Dārul-Kutubil-'Ilmiyyah, Beirut, 2004)

At this point when she saw the determination of her son, she started to eat again. There are numerous other incidents in history which demonstrate the extreme love and devotion of the companions of the Holy Prophet[sa].

دامانِ نگہ تنگ و گلِ حسنِ تو بسیار

The reach of my sight is limited,
Yet the flowers of your beauty are endless.

COUPLET 12

قَدْ وَدَّعُوْا أَهْوَاءَهُمْ وَنُفُوْسَهُمْ
وَ تَبَرَّءُوْا مِنْ كُلِّ نَشَبٍ فَانِ

They bid farewell to their base desires, and self-indulgence;
They discarded all their material belongings.

When people accepted Islam they not only sacrificed their personal desires, but actually bid farewell to their own selves. They no longer maintained any individual inclinations towards themselves. In reality, a person becomes a true Muslim at this very stage, when one is willing to sacrifice his life in the way of Allāh, and devotes his being for the sake of Allāh, and then prostrates towards the Beloved God with such truthfulness and devotion that nothing else exists other than the Beloved. It is at this stage that a person's feelings reach a kind of death. All faculties and powers of spirit function solely for the sake of Allāh. With every movement and pause, the life and death of a Muslim belongs to Allāh alone.

اسلام چیز کیا ہے خدا کے لئے فنا
ترکِ رضائے خویش پئے مرضیٔ خدا

Islām is nothing but dying for the sake of Allāh,
And abandoning all one's desires to fulfil the desires of Allāh.

(*Barāhīn-e-Aḥmadiyya, Rūḥānī Khazā'in*, vol. 21, p. 18)

The Promised Messiah[as] writes in his book 'The Philosophy of the Teachings of Islam:'

اسلام کیا چیز ہے۔ وہی جلتی ہوئی آگ جو ہماری سفلی زندگی کو بھسم کر کے اور ہمارے باطل معبودوں کو جلا کر سچے اور پاک معبود کے آگے ہماری جان اور ہمارا مال اور ہماری آبرو کی قربانی پیش کرتی ہے۔ ایسے چشمہ میں داخل ہو کر ہم ایک نئی زندگی کا پانی پیتے ہیں اور ہماری تمام روحانی قوتیں خدا سے یوں پیوند پکڑتی ہیں جیسا کہ ایک رشتہ دوسرے رشتہ سے پیوند کیا جاتا ہے۔ بجلی کی آگ کی طرح ایک آگ ہمارے اندر سے نکلتی ہے اور ایک آگ اوپر سے ہم پر اترتی ہے ان دونوں شعلوں کے ملنے سے ہماری تمام ہواؤ ہوس اور غیر اللہ کی محبت بھسم ہو جاتی ہے۔ اور ہم اپنی پہلی زندگی سے مر جاتے ہیں اس حالت کا نام قرآن شریف کی رُو سے اسلام ہے۔ اسلام سے ہمارے نفسانی جذبات کو موت آتی ہے۔ اور پھر دعا سے ہم از سر نو زندہ ہوتے ہیں۔

> What is Islam? It is a fire that burns our sinful life and our false idols and presents the sacrifice of our life, wealth and honour before the True and Sacred God. We enter into this fountain and we drink water for a new life. All of our spiritual capacities unite with God in a manner just as a relative is connected to another. In the likeness of lightness, one fire comes forth from within us and another descends from above and when these two meet they burn the love for worldly gains and false idols, and we experience a death before our lives are over. This is the condition, which according to the Holy Qur'ān is referred to as Islam. Islam brings death to our worldly desires and then through prayer we are born again.
>
> (*Philosophy of the Teachings of Islam, Rūḥānī Khazā'in*, vol. 10, p. 394)

In essence, the companions of the Holy Prophet[sa] did not care for their wealth or their properties, but preoccupied themselves entirely with the practice of Islam. Once they received the commandment to migrate, they left their homes without regard for their relatives and worldly riches.

Ḥaḍrat Ṣuḥaib[ra] was a rich businessman of Mecca and was considered fairly well off. In spite of his wealth and his having been granted freedom, the Quraish would beat him until he would fall unconscious. When the Holy Prophet[sa] migrated to Medina, Ḥaḍrat Ṣuḥaib[ra] decided to migrate as well. However, the people of Mecca stopped him and told him that he could not take his wealth with him because he had earned it in Mecca. In this way they had forbidden him to leave the city. Ṣuḥaib[ra] asked if he could depart on the condition that he relinquished all his wealth. To this they agreed and he handed over all his wealth, and arrived in Medina empty handed. When he visited the Holy Prophet[sa] and explained what had happened, the Holy Prophet[sa] responded, 'Ṣuḥaib, this transaction you made is more profitable than your last hundred deals.'

(*Al-Mustadrak Lil-Ḥākim, Kitābu Ma'rifatiṣ-Ṣaḥābah,* Dhikru Ṣuhaib bin Sanān, vol. 6, p. 2089–2090, Ḥadīth no. 5706, Maktabah Nazāril-Muṣṭafal-Bāz, Saudia Arabia edition 2000)

He meant that although Ṣuḥaib[ra] received money from his previous deals, he received a better bargain this time by receiving faith.

COUPLET 13

ظَهَرَتْ عَلَيْهِمْ بَيِّنَاتُ رَسُوْلِهِمْ
فَتَمَزَّقَ الْاَهْوَاءُ كَالْاَوْثَانِ

When the clear signs of the truth of their Prophet became manifest upon them,
Their base desires were shattered to pieces like smashed idols.

The greatest obstacles that a person faces in the way of accepting truth are those drives and desires which degrade one below the status of a human being. Sometimes people worship their desires just as a pagan worships idols. Allāh says in the Holy Qur'ān:

أَمْ تَحْسَبُ أَنَّ أَكْثَرَهُمْ يَسْمَعُونَ أَوْ يَعْقِلُونَ ۚ إِنْ هُمْ إِلَّا كَالْأَنْعَامِ بَلْ هُمْ أَضَلُّ سَبِيلًا

Hast thou seen him who takes his own evil desire for his god? Couldst thou then be a guardian over him? Dost thou think that most of them hear or understand? They are only like cattle; nay they are worst astray from the path. (*al-Furqān*, 25:44–45)

In these verses, Allāh is referring to those people who have taken their desires as idols. Allāh says in the above verse that most of these people have lost their human qualities such as hearing and understanding, and He says they are just like animals, some being even worse.

In this couplet, worldly desires are likened to idols, composing a very beautiful and accurate metaphor. The fact is that Allāh made human beings His vicegerents in the earth and He has said:

وَلَقَدْ كَرَّمْنَا بَنِيْٓ اٰدَمَ

Meaning, 'Indeed, We have honoured the children of Adam.' (*Banī Isrā'īl*, 17:71)

Allah has subdued for mankind the sky, earth, sun, moon, stars, canals, rivers, oceans, cliffs and high mountain tops. In short, everything found in the heavens and the earth has been created for the benefit of human beings. Thus, a human being is subjected to Allāh and the rest of creation is subjected to human beings.

A poet with profound thoughts about the operation of the universe has said in his Persian couplet addressing humanity:

ابر و باد ومہ و خورشید و فلک در کارند
تا تو نانے بکف آری و بغفلت نخوری
ہمہ از بہرِ تو سر گشتہ و فرماں بردار
شرطِ انصاف نہ باشد کہ تو فرماں نہ بری

The rain, the wind, the moon, the sun and the skies are all engaged in their proper course at all times,
So that you can make a living, and not be confined to a state of laziness or inactivity.

They are all labouring for you and are obedient,
And therefore justice demands that you be obedient too.

(*Tauḍīḥ-e-Marām, Rūḥānī Khazā'in,* vol. 3, p. 85)

In spite of all this, a group of people continues to insult humanity with their own hands. Some of them prostrate in front of stones, while some stand in prayer to the sun. They consider the sun, among other things, to have the power of fulfilling their needs. Allāh has given the example of a person indulging in *shirk* [polytheism], as one who falls from heaven to earth because a person guilty of *shirk* desires to be a servant despite being created as one who is served, and inclines towards lowliness instead of moving towards heights.

The victory of Mecca is also a clear proof of the truth of the Holy Prophet[sa]. When the Holy Prophet[sa] victoriously entered the Ka'bah with his 10,000 companions, the first task he performed was to demolish the 360 idols that lay there into pieces. He thus opened the door for humanity to rise from the pit of degradation into the heights of dignity, which is its intended destination. May the peace and blessings of Allāh be upon the Holy Prophet[sa].

Not only did the destruction of idols serve as the means by which human beings were elevated to a lofty station, but it helped people destroy their worldly desires, promote their spirituality, and develop bonds between them and Allāh.

COUPLET 14

فِيْ وَقْتِ تَرْوِيْقِ اللَّيَالِيْ نُوِّرُوْا
وَاللّٰهُ نَجَّاهُمْ مِّنَ الطُّوْفَانِ

They became enlightened in the pitch darkness of night;
And Allah saved them from being engulfed in a raging storm of torment.

In this couplet the condition at the time of the Holy Prophet[sa] is described as a very deep darkness. This fact is acknowledged by all historians, whether Muslim or not. During this particular era the whole world was in its dark ages. (The same discussion applies here as under Couplet 1 of this Qaṣīdah.)

COUPLET 15

قَدْ هَاضَهُمْ ظُلْمُ الْأُنَاسِ وَضَيْمُهُمْ
فَتَثَبَّتُوْا بِعِنَايَةِ الْمَنَّانِ

The fury and wrath of the opponents attempted to grind them to dust;
But the mercy of their Beneficent Lord sustained them and they remained steadfast.

In the early days of Islam, the cruelties perpetrated against the believers are rarely found in previous prophet's times. Purkāsh Devī who was a *Parcharik* of *Brahmu Samāj* [a Hindu sect] in Lahore writes in his book Sawāneḥ 'Umrī Ḥaḍrat Muḥammad Ṣāḥib (The Life of Muḥammad[sa]):

> Those helpless believers had a mountain of atrocities fall upon them. People would seize them and take them to a strip of wilderness and lay them upon the hot sands and place stone slabs upon their chests. They would squirm about because of the heat and their tongues would hang out, being pressed out by the heavy weight upon them. Many of them died from this torture. Among those persecuted was a person named 'Ammār. Actually, because of the patience and determination he displayed against his persecutors he should be called Ḥaḍrat 'Ammār. They would tie him up and let him lie on rocky gravel area and order him to insult Muḥammad. This same treatment was given to his aging father. His mother whose name was Sumaiyyah could not bear this

cruelty to her husband. She would plead for their lives. The result was that this innocent believing woman, who was witnessing cruelties against her husband and son, was stripped and given such horrible treatment that it is shameful for me to describe it. Finally, as a result of this extreme punishment she gave up her life.

(*Sawāneḥ 'Umrī Ḥaḍrat Muḥammad*[sa] *Ṣāḥib Bānī-e-Islām*, Shardhiay Parkāsh Dev Jī, p. 37–38, Publisher Narā'in Datt Sehgal and Sons, Lahore, 10th edition)

Under a well planned scheme, atrocities were committed against the believers for thirteen years. The Promised Messiah[as] has written:

The faithful of God and the best of human beings were cut into pieces by the swords of those vicious animals with great cruelty, and the orphans, the helpless and poor women were slaughtered in the streets. Even then the clear commandment from Allāh was that they should not fight against this evil. These true believers did exactly the same. Their streets turned red with their blood but they did not retaliate. They were slaughtered like animals but they did not utter a word. The holy and sacred Prophet of God, upon whom the blessings are sent from the Heavens and the Earth, was barraged by rocks and his blood was shed, but as a mountain of truth and determination, he endured all of these torments with an open and loving heart. The mischief of the opponents continually grew worse because of the patience and humility of the believers. They looked upon this pure group of people as their prey. Then God became furious at the mischievous oppressors for He did not want cruelty and mischief to exceed the limits and came to the

> help of His servants. Allāh announced to His servants in the Holy Qur'ān that I am seeing what is happening to you and I give you permission to respond. I am the Almighty God and I will not let the cruel go without punishment. This is the commandment that was given the name jihad.
>
> (*The British Government & Jihad, Rūḥānī Khazā'in*, vol. 7, p. 5–6)

Allāh testifies in the Holy Qur'ān that the believers were wronged:

أُذِنَ لِلَّذِيْنَ يُقٰتَلُوْنَ بِاَنَّهُمْ ظُلِمُوْا ؕ وَ اِنَّ اللّٰهَ عَلٰى نَصْرِهِمْ لَقَدِيْرُ ﴿٣٩﴾ ۙ الَّذِيْنَ
اُخْرِجُوْا مِنْ دِيَارِهِمْ بِغَيْرِ حَقٍّ اِلَّاۤ اَنْ يَّقُوْلُوْا رَبُّنَا اللّٰهُ ؕ...

> **Permission (to fight) is given to those against whom war is made, because they have been wronged-and Allāh indeed has power to help them. Those who have been driven out from their homes unjustly only because they said, 'Our Lord is Allāh'...(*al-Ḥajj*, 22:40–41)**

This illustrates that not only were they considered to have been wronged in the view of Allāh, but in the eyes of the public as well. Therefore, their steadfastness was due to the special favour of Allāh.

COUPLET 16

نَهَبَ اللِّئَامُ نُشُوبَهُمْ وَ عَقَارَهُمْ
فَتَهَلَّلُوْا بِجَوَاهِرِ الْفُرْقَانِ

The despicable and accursed of the earth looted all their belongings;
But their faces gleamed upon receiving the pearls of the Qur'ān.

The opponents of Islam confiscated and destroyed all of the assets which belonged to the companions, both movable and immovable. Nevertheless, the companions were much contented to receive the precious jewel of the Qur'ān. They considered it priceless and everlasting. It was a treasure none could seize from them, being immune from theft and corruption. Wherever they took this valuable treasure, be it a tribe or nation, they were granted respect and honour, and they received further assurance from their Creator and Master, Allāh, in this very world that He was well pleased with them.[5]

[5] *al-Mā'idah*, 5:120

COUPLET 17

كَسَحُوْا بُيُوْتَ نُفُوْسِهِمْ وَ تَبَادَرُوْا
لِتَمَتُّعِ الْاِيْقَانِ وَ الْاِيْمَانِ

They thoroughly cleansed their souls of all impurities,
And moved forward to gain the wealth of unflinching fait.

In this couplet another virtue of the companions of the Holy Prophet[sa] is described. They were well aware that the wealth of faith and certainty could not be attained without the cleansing of the inner self. In accordance with this, they cleansed and purified their hearts.

One event illustrates the extent to which they would purify themselves. It involves a man who committed fornication. Although he knew the punishment for the act was stoning, he presented himself before the Holy Prophet[sa] and confessed his sin. He told the Holy Prophet[sa] that he had become unclean by committing the sin and did not want a blemish upon him. He then requested the application of the law against him for cleansing. The Holy Prophet[sa] asked him if he was in his senses to which he replied affirmatively. After having repeated his confession four times, the Holy Prophet[sa] declared the punishment of fornication upon him.[6] This incident provides us an idea of how conscious the companions

[6] *Kitābu Sunanil-Kubrā Lin-Nasa'ī*, Kitābur-Rajm, Bābu Kaifal-I'tirāfu Biz-Zinā'i, vol. 4, p. 276, Ḥadīth no. 7163, Dārul-Kutubil-'Ilmiyyah, Beirut, 2001

of the Holy Prophet[sa] truly were of keeping themselves clean and pure.

COUPLETS 18 and 19

قَامُوْا بِإِقْدَامِ الرَّسُوْلِ بِغَزْوِهِمْ
كَالْعَاشِقِ الْمَشْغُوْفِ فِي الْمِيْدَانِ

In battle, they stood with the Messenger in ranks.
Intoxicated in love, they marched forward to the battlefield.

فَدَمُ الرِّجَالِ لِصِدْقِهِمْ فِيْ حُبِّهِمْ
تَحْتَ السُّيُوْفِ أُرِيْقَ كَالْقُرْبَانِ

The blood of sincere lovers was shed under the sword;
Like the blood of sacrificed animals flowing under the knife,

In these two couplets the central theme revolves around the complete obedience of the companions, their steadfastness in battle, and their willingness to sacrifice their own lives.

In the Battle of Badr the Muslim soldiers numbered 313 while their Meccan opponents numbered 1,000. However, the state of the Muslims was strengthened by their devotion, love and faith. This was best described by one of their opponents, ʻUmair bin Wahab, who was assigned the task of estimating the size of the Muslim army. The Meccans were delighted when ʻUmair advised them that the Muslims were limited to about 300 to 325 soldiers. Fearing over-confidence on the part of the Meccans, 'Umair warned them, 'O Meccans, my advice to you is not to fight with them because I have not seen men mounted upon camels, but death.' He meant to say that every Muslim on the battlefield was prepared to die and would not accept defeat without a fierce fight.[7]

The love displayed by the companions on the battlefield is simply remarkable. Initially in the Battle of Uḥud, the Muslims were on their way to victory. However, due to a small group of Muslim soldiers disobeying the command of the Holy Prophet[sa], the situation turned into one of defeat. The enemy archers ascended onto the hills and launched waves of arrows at the Holy Prophet[sa]. Ḥaḍrat Ṭalḥah extended his hand to shield the face of the Holy Prophet[sa] from these arrows. Arrow after arrow pierced into the hand of Ṭalḥah[ra], but this valiant companion would not move his hand. So many arrows penetrated his hand that it was disabled and later amputated.

Years later during the caliphate of Ḥaḍrat 'Alī[ra], when the Muslims were fighting one another, a man offensively remarked to Ḥaḍrat Ṭalḥah as the one-handed. Another companion rebuked the man saying, 'Yes, he is the one-handed, but a very blessed one-handed indeed. You should know that Ṭalḥah's hand was amputated because he used it to shield the sacred face of the Holy Prophet[sa].'

---

[7] *As-Sīratun-Nabawiyyah,* Ibni Hishām, Dhikru Ru'yā 'Ātikah bint 'Abdil-Muṭṭalib..., p. 424–425, Dārul-Kutubil-'Ilmiyyah, Beirut, 2001

A person asked Ṭalḥah after the Battle of Uḥud, 'When the arrows were striking your hand did you not feel pain and cry out as a result?'

Ḥaḍrat Ṭalḥah replied, 'Yes, it was painful and I wanted to cry out, but I did not utter a word for fear that my hand might shake back and leave the Prophet's face exposed to the next arrow.'[8]

During the Battle of Uḥud there is another incident involving a lover of the Holy Prophet[sa]. After sustaining an injury the Holy Prophet[sa] fell into a ditch and many companions who were trying to protect him were martyred in the process. The Holy Prophet[sa] was covered by their bodies as they fell upon him one by one. The opponents started yelling that the Holy Prophet[sa] had been killed.

Upon hearing this news Ḥaḍrat 'Umar[ra] broke down and sitting upon a stone, burst into tears. Another companion, Ḥaḍrat Mālik, who was under the impression that the Muslim army had won the battle, and was unaware it had turned into defeat, was eating dates as he passed by Ḥaḍrat 'Umar[ra]. Mālik asked 'Umar[ra] why he was crying. 'Umar[ra] replied that the Holy Prophet[sa] had been martyred. Ḥaḍrat Mālik[ra] then questioned 'Umar[ra], 'If this news is correct, why are you sitting here crying? We should go to the same world our beloved has gone.'

Ḥaḍrat Mālik[ra] addressed the last date he was about to eat and said, 'Between Mālik and Paradise you are the only thing that stands in between.'

---

[8] *As-Sīratul-Ḥalabiyyah,* 'Allāmah Abil-Faraj Nūrid-Dīn, vol. 2, p. 324, Bābu Dhikri Maghāzīhī (Ghazwatu Uḥud), Dārul-Kutubil-'Ilmiyyah, Beirut, 2002

He then threw away the date, took out his sword and charged the opposing army of 3,000 soldiers. The opponents were amazed by the zeal and fervour with which he was fighting. He was eventually injured and fell. Even in this condition he continued attacking the soldiers coming near him with his sword. Finally, many opponents pounced upon him simultaneously and cut his body into pieces. When they were through, they had cut him into seventy pieces making him unrecognizable. His sister later identified his body by pointing to a mark on his finger.

There are so many other exemplary displays of love, steadfastness and faithfulness of the companions in battle that it is impossible to cover them in a book as small as this.

The companions firmly believed the saying of the Holy Prophet[sa]:

أَنَّ الْجَنَّةَ تَحْتَ ظِلَالِ السُّيُوفِ

Meaning, "Paradise lies beneath the shadow of swords."

(*Ṣaḥīḥul-Bukhārī*, Kitābul-Jihādi Was-Siyar, Bābul-Jannati Taḥta Bāriqatis-Suyūf, Ḥadīth no.. 2818)

They had a clear understanding engraved upon their hearts that Paradise could not be earned by a life of material luxury, but by expending life under the drawn out swords of opposition. The fact that they sacrificed their lives in the battlefield proved to be a true sacrifice in the cause of Islam. Not only did they achieve the status of martyrdom and nearness to Allāh, their sacrifices became a means for others to attain nearness to God, and continue to do so. The blood they shed in the battlefields did not merely benefit them as individuals, but served as nourishment to the garden of Islam. It made that garden green and filled it with flourishing fruits.

COUPLET 20

جَاءُوْكَ مَنْهُوْبِيْنَ كَالْعُرْيَانِ
فَسَتَرْتَهُمْ بِمَلَاحِفِ الْإِيْمَانِ

They came to you looted and naked,
And you clothed them with the cloak of faith.

Arabs before the advent of Islam were devoid of every type of good and indulged in every type of evil. There was no nation on earth more ignorant and more arrogant than them. They lacked civilization and tradition. They did not have any signs of righteousness or fear of Allāh in them. All they craved was fame and glory. Their condition was of a people who had been robbed of all their valuables and who did not have anything to cover their bodies with.

In these conditions, O my lord and master, they presented themselves to you and you gave them the wealth of Islam and you gave them the cloth of righteousness and covered them with fabrics of faith. You transformed them into people who wanted to leave all others behind in the performance of virtuous acts. And it was in following your footsteps that faith and righteousness became their attire.

From this couplet through 39 is the mention of this great revolution that took place amongst the nation of Arabia by the efforts of the Holy Prophet[sa].

COUPLET 21

صَادَفْتَهُمْ قَوْمًا كَرَوْثٍ ذِلَّةً
فَجَعَلْتَهُمْ كَسَبِيْكَةِ الْعِقْيَانِ

You found them dirty like a heap of dung;
And transformed them into a piece of pure gold.

In this couplet the condition of the Arabian people before the advent of Islam has been compared to dung, meaning, they were shameless. They had no value amongst the nations of the world but, O my master, your nearness, your friendship and by following you they became the likes of gold medallions. They achieved such position and status among the nations of the world that it is futile to find a comparable example in history, either before or after.

COUPLET 22

حَتّٰى انْثَنٰى بَرٌّ كَمِثْلِ حَدِيْقَةٍ
عَذْبِ الْمَوَارِدِ مُثْمِرِ الْاَغْصَانِ

And the wilderness of Arabia was transformed into such a garden;
The streams of which are pleasant and sweet, and the trees of which are laden with fruits.

In this couplet the condition of the Arabs is likened to a desert with no life, water or greenery. Not only does this desert lack anything attractive, interesting or any place for peace and comfort, but trouble, destruction and death is apparent everywhere. From this desert you could not get anything to eat or drink, not even a place for shade. However, with the advent of the Holy Prophet[sa] this awful and terrorizing desert was transformed into an attractive, beautiful garden which provides pleasure. In this garden there are canals of pure and clear water and its green and fresh trees are such that hearts impulsively incline to it. The flowers growing in this garden emanate such fragrance that one's soul gets enchanted with its aroma. The tongue and body enjoy the taste of its fruits to the extent that there is no equal.

In the garden of Islam, one of the beautiful fruits was Ḥaḍrat 'Umar[ra]. When he visited Jerusalem, he entered a very respectable church upon the invitation of its priests. During his visit, the time of prayer came and the priests requested him to perform his prayers in the church but he refused by saying that if he prayed in the church, he feared that future Muslims may use that as an excuse to take over the church and convert it into a mosque and this would prove to be very painful for the Christians. He walked out of the church and offered his prayers near the stairway at which place there is a small mosque now.[9]

Another beautiful fruit of the garden of Islam was Abū 'Ubaidah[ra]. He received orders from the headquarters that Muslim armies should move out from the city of Ḥamṣ and other towns of Syria and move into another sector. Ḥaḍrat Abū 'Ubaidah[ra] called the leaders of that city and informed them that they would be moving out and would not be able to provide them protection, therefore the *jizyah* [protection tax] that was collected in that year would be returned. The Christians of the city were in tears to see this honourable treatment and expressed that they could not imagine even a Christian government treating them in this manner. They prayed and hoped that he (Abū 'Ubaidah[ra]) would return to their city.[10]

In essence, the fruits of this garden of Islam were so tasty and pleasant that they were unique and there was nothing like them.

---

[9] *Al-Khulafā'ur-Rāshidīn,* Qudūmu 'Umar Ilash-Shāmi, Dhikru 'Ahdi Ahli Baitil-Muqaddas, p. 202, Dārul-Kutubil-'Arabiyy, Beirut (2004)

[10] *Siyarus-Ṣaḥābah*, vol. 2, p. 171–172, published by Idārah Islāmiyāt, Lahore

COUPLET 23

عَادَتْ بِلَادُ الْعَرَبِ نَحْوَ نَضَارَةٍ
بَعْدَ الْوَجَی وَ الْمَحْلِ وَ الْخُسْرَانِ

The towns of Arabia awoke to life once again;
Leaving the days of death and drought behind.

The cities of the Arabian nation were depicted a picture of desolation, desertion and famine. There was no hope of any benefit or usefulness from them. Desolation, abomination and clouds of evil were covering them and it seemed that death and destruction would prevail any minute. But O rain of mercy, with your coming all the dry land disappeared. The parched earth was replaced with green foliage. Desolation and abomination disappeared. The deserts transformed into gardens. Desolate places became full of life. Hustle, bustle and springtime festivities appeared everywhere.

COUPLET 24

كَانَ الْحِجَازُ مَغَازِلَ الْغِزْلَانِ
فَجَعَلْتَهُمْ فَانِيْنَ فِی الرَّحْمَانِ

The men of Ḥijāz, who were given to the love of women;
You made them satiated in love of the Gracious God.

At this part of the Qaṣīdah there is a reference to some of the social evils that were prevalent among the Arabs. These evils are of such nature that once a nation adopts them, they are destroyed morally and spiritually, and it is very difficult to bring about reformation. These evils are lewdness, drinking, and music. According to the Talmūd[11] these three types of sins or evils were rampant among the people of Lot. Since they could not reform themselves they were destroyed. Nowadays these three evils have taken root in European nations as well. Since their governments have some control through their laws, they are punished to some extent for these evils. Some governments are trying to eliminate some of these evils but they are unsuccessful. The problem is that sinful activities are publicized openly in stories and writings, and in free newspapers, magazines and print articles, and this arouses and stimulates the sexual urges of people. There is no control over any of these publications. Actors and singers, whether men or women, are given the highest respect in these societies. Their scholars and writers admit that obscenity and adultery have taken hold of their society and it is impossible to remove it.

These three evils were part and parcel of the culture and civilization of the Arabs and they used to boast and recite verses about these things in their gatherings with pride. By way of example, a very famous Arab poet, Labīd bin Rabī'ah, says in his couplets addressing his beloved:

[11] *The Tālmūd*, by H. Polano, p. 45, London, Frederick Warne & Co.

بل انت لاتدرين كم من ليلةٍ

طلق لذيذ لهوها وندامها

قد بتّ سامرها وغاية تاجر

وافيت اذ رفعت وعزّ مدامها

اغلى السباء بكلّ ادكن عاتق

او جونة قدحت وفض ختامها

وبصبوح صافية وجذب كرينة

بمؤتر تأتأله ابهامها

O my love, you have no idea as to how many pleasant nights I have spent among my friends in which we had great times of drinking. How many times I came to the tavern and we set out drinking and we drank so much that they were running out of it. I always bid the highest on the old whiskey in an antique bottle or wine from a big pot of which the seal has just been broken. I have been enchanted so many times by the clean and pure wine in the morning and the music and the sound of the strings played by a young woman.

(*Sharḥul-Mu'allaqātil-'Ashri,* Mu'allaqah Labīd bin Rabī'ah, p. 102–103, Dāru Iḥyā'it-Turāthil-'Arabiyy)

In the same manner, another poet, Ṭurfah bin 'Abdil-Bakarī, writes in his poetry:

فلولا ثلاث من عيشة الفتی

وجدّک احفل متی تام عوّدی

فمنهنّ سبقی العاذلات بشربة

کُمیت متی ما تغل بالماء تزبد

و کرّی اذا نادی المضاف محنبا

کسید الغضی نبهته المتورد

وتقصیر یوم الدجن والدجن معجب

ببهکنة تحت الخباء المعمّد

If I died because of any of the following three then I would not care about my death at all. One of them is that if I was the winner in drinking red wine – the kind that foams on the top if you mix it with water and boil it. Secondly if I am riding a fast horse to go help a terrified person against whom a cruelty has been committed. Thirdly if I am with a beautiful young, healthy girl under a tent, which has pillars in it, and the day is pleasant with clouds and has been shortened [extending the night].

(*Sharḥul-Mu'allaqātil-'Ashri,* Mu'allaqah Ṭurfah bin 'Abdil-Bakarī, p. 53–54, Dāru Iḥyā'it-Turāthil-'Arabiyy)

Another example is the poet of Arabia from the era of *jāhiliyyah* [ignorance] Imra'ul-Qais:

وبيضة خدر لا يرام خباءها

تمتعت من لهوبها غير معجل

تجاوزت احراساً اليها ومعشرا

حراصا عليّ لو يسرّون مقتلي

فجئت وقد نضّت لنوم ثيابها

لدى الستر الّا لبسة المتفضل

خرجت بها تمشي تجرّ وراءنا

على اثرينا ذيل مرط مرحّل

فلما اجزنا ساحة الحيّ وانتحى

بنا بطن خبت ذى حقاف عقنقل

هصرت بفودى رأسها فتمايلت

عليّ هفيم الكشح ريّا المخلخل

There are many beautiful young girls who are not chased into their tents, but I have encountered them and have satisfied myself by playing with them. In these ventures I have passed through many guards and groups of people; if they had caught me, they would have killed me. I went to them at the time when they had taken off their clothes and only had their nightgowns on.

I do not consider it proper to translate the rest of the couplets.

The publication of obscenity and lewdness were done openly and people used to be very proud of them. This was the kind of poetry that was considered to be excellent literature and they used to hang these on the *Ka'bah*.

As these evils entered amongst the Christians they lost spirituality as well. A very famous Christian poet of the 1st century *hijrah* named Akhṭal in his following couplet refers to himself, but actually depicts the real condition of the Christians of that time:

بَانَ الشباب وربما عللته

بالغانيات وبالشراب الاصهب

I have lost my youth and I have tried to recover it by the use of red wine and beautiful young women.

(*Dīwānu Akhṭal*, p. 204, Dārul-Kitābul-'Arabiyy, Beirut, 1994)

In this couplet, Akhṭal who was very respected and honourable among his people has actually drawn a picture of the lives of his people. He has admitted to the true evils of his people, which are excessive drinking and womanizing.[12]

In essence the three evils, i.e., womanizing and drinking, which are tied to lewdness, and music, the latter two being subservient to the first two, are the entire basis for luxury and voluptuousness.

This couplet mentions the evil of the Arabs, that they exhibited unbridled love for women. It seems they could not eliminate it

[12]A Summary of *Nūrul-Qur'ān*, no. 1, *Rūḥānī Khazā'in*, vol. 9, p. 344

from their minds. They were free souls with plenty of time on their hands and were therefore preoccupied in indulging themselves.

In this couplet, beautiful women have been called *ghazlān*, because the Arabian people used to compare them to the grace and beauty of the white deer. The poet Akhṭal writes about his church in the following couplet:

ان من يدخل الكنيسة يوما

يلقى فيها جآذرا وظباء

> If you go in my church someday you will really enjoy it, seeing some young and beautiful deer [meaning women].
>
> (*Mughnil-Labīb*, vol. 1, p. 34, Dāru Iḥyā'it-Turāthil- 'Arabiyy, 2001 edition)

O my beloved prophet, the people of Ḥijāz who were absorbed in the love of beautiful women fell in love with God because of their association with you. Their thoughts, mental patterns, feelings, actions, their sitting, standing, eating, drinking, their words, their intentions and desires all became subservient to the Will of God. These same people handed themselves over to God as if they had died and attained a new life.

COUPLET 25

شَيْـئَانِ كَانَ الْقَوْمُ عُمْيًا فِيْهِمَا
حَشْوُ الْعُقَارِ وَكَثْرَةُ النِّسْوَانِ

Only two additions had made the Arabs blind:
Wine and women were all that they sought.

In this couplet the second evil is mentioned which is drinking alcohol. The excessive number of women is in reference to those who were dancers, singers and those involved in sexual activities. The Arabian nation was involved in both of these evils from head to toe without regard for the outcome.

COUPLET 26

أَمَّا النِّسَاءُ فَحُرِّمَتْ إِنْكَاحُهَا
زَوْجًا لَّهُ التَّحْرِيْمُ فِى الْقُرْاٰنِ

Concerning women clear commandments were laid down;
Prohibiting men marrying those who were prohibited by the Qur'ān

To stop the evil of immoral sexual relations, the law was declared in the Holy Qur'ān that no man or woman would have sexual relations with such a person who fell in the category specifically mentioned in the Holy Qur'ān, and sexual relations with others was permitted in the case of marriage only. In *Sūrah an-Nisā'* Allāh says:

> **And marry not those women whom your fathers married except that which has already passed, it is a thing foul and hateful and an evil way. Forbidden to you are your mothers and your daughters and your sisters and your father's sisters and your mother's sisters and brother's daughters and sister's daughters and your foster mothers that have given you suck, and your foster sisters and the mothers of your wives and your stepdaughters who are your wards by your wives whom you have gone in - but if you have not gone in unto them, there shall be no sin upon you - and the wives of your sons that are from your loins and it is forbidden to you to have two sisters together except what has already passed, surely Allāh is Most Forgiving, Merciful. And forbidden to you are married women except such as your right hand possesses. This Allāh has enjoined on you. And allowed to you are those beyond that, that you seek them by means of your property, marrying them properly and not committing fornication.** (*an-Nisā'*, 4:23–25)

The Holy Qur'ān prescribes a punishment for any man or woman who creates an unlawful relationship with the opposite sex.

COUPLET 27

وَجَعَلْتَ دَسْكَرَةَ الْمُدَامِ مُخَرَّبًا
وَ أَزَلْتَ حَانَتَهَا مِنَ الْبُلْدَانِ

And you laid waste the drinking places;
And you closed down the drinking of all the towns.

The couplet mentions a great accomplishment of the Holy Prophet[sa], which was actually a miracle. A drinking epidemic was prevalent amongst the Arabs and every one of them enjoyed talking about it. They used to boast about drinking and getting drunk. Their poetry was full of praise for drinking.

A poet by the name Labīd bin Rabī'ah, says in one of his couplets:

بادرت حاجتها الدجاج بسحرة
لاعلّ منها حين هبّ نيامها

I was drinking in the morning even before the rooster awoke, not to hide my drinking from people but that I could take pride and boast to the people when I greeted them in the bar that morning, that they were drinking for the first time and I for the second.

(*Sharḥul-Mu'allaqātil-'Ashri,* Mu'allaqah Labīd bin Rabī'ah, p. 103, Dāru Iḥyā'it-Turāthil-'Arabiyy)

Another poet, 'Amr bin Kulthūm Taghlabī, says in his poetry:

الاهبّی بصحنک فصبحینا
ولاتبقی خمور الاندرینا
وکاس قد شربت ببعلبک
واخریٰ فی دمشق وقاصرینا

O my love, pick up the glass and give me all the liquor that has been made in the town of Andarīn, and make sure that nothing is left in the cellar. I tasted the wine from the town Ba'labek, and Damascus and I used to drink in the place Qāṣirīn.

(*Sharḥul-Mu'allaqātil-'Ashri,* Mu'allaqah 'Amr bin Kulthūm, p. 113–114, Dāru Iḥyā'it-Turāthil-'Arabiyy)

In the ancient religions, such as Judaism and Christianity, drinking of wine was allowed in one form or another. However, Christians developed the habit of drinking more than others. Even in this age, Christian nations are the centre of wine production and drinking. Alcohol consumption increased in every country the Christian powers took over.

In the current age, a powerful nation like the United States, which is considered to be the leader in methods of governance, worldly power and wealth, made laws against the production and consumption of alcohol. They attempted to remove this disgrace from their country through the consolidated efforts of police, military and department of taxation, but they failed. As a matter of fact, the consumption of alcohol increased after the passing of these laws.

Similarly, the government of India in 1956 tried to pass laws to place partial controls on alcohol production. What came out of this was reported by the reporter of an Urdu newspaper *Nawā-e-Waqt*:

> Since April 1, 1956, there is a partial control on the consumption of alcohol in Delhi. There were seven places in the metropolitan area, producing local wine, which were closed down. Only three places were allowed to operate outside the metropolitan area. In western bars new restrictions were placed on the hours of operation. The alcohol was allowed from noon to 3pm and between 7pm and 10pm, and was allowed only with meals. Before April 1st bars were required to close on Tuesdays. Now they are required to be closed on Tuesdays as well as on Fridays. However, the interesting news is, in spite of these controls, the consumption of alcohol went up instead of going down. It has been reported that compared to April of last year, in the city of Delhi, the consumption of alcohol was higher by 634 gallons of hard liquor and 2,559 gallons of beer. There was a noticeable increase in the licensed places which sell local alcohol. Actually the increase in these locations was greater. In April of 1955, they sold 1,800 bottles, but in 1956, in the first week of April alone, they sold 3,000.
>
> (*Nawā'-e-Waqt, July 10, 1956*, p. 2, Maktūb-e-Delhi)

The effect of the holy personality of the Holy Prophet[sa] was such that in the 4th year after *hijrah*, when he announced that the drinking of alcohol was no longer permissible, the Muslims gave up drinking immediately. It has been reported in a *Ḥadīth*, that when this was announced in the city of Medina, a drinking party was going on at the house of one of the Muslims of Medina. The first round was in progress and the second about to begin. When the announcement was made in the street that due to the commandment of Allāh, the Holy Prophet[sa] has forbidden the drinking of alcohol, a person in the party stood up and said that he hears the sound of a pronouncement against the drinking of alcohol. Let us get the details. But another person stood up and shattered the keg into pieces and said let us obey the commandment first and then ascertain the details.[13]

It has also been reported in a *Ḥadīth* that on the day the commandment of prohibition was announced, wine was flowing from the streets of Medina like water. All the Muslims who heard the announcement never drank again. Only one announcement was enough to remove the chronic disease of drinking from the Arabian nation. As a result of this bars were deserted and liquor stores were locked up. There was no more production of alcohol or drinking.

This immediate transformation which took place because of the holy powers of the Holy Prophet[sa] is such a majestic, sublime and exalted revolution that no equal to this can be found in any nation either before the advent of the Holy Prophet[sa] or after.

[13] *Ṣaḥīḥ Muslim,* Kitābul-Ashribah, Bābu Taḥrīmil-Khamri..., Ḥadīth no. 5131, 5321

COUPLET 28

كَمْ شَارِبٍ بِالرَّشْفِ دَنًّا طَافِحًا
فَجَعَلْتَهُ فِي الدِّيْنِ كَالنَّشْوَانِ

Many were those who were given to boozing;
But you made them drunk with the wine of faith.

Just as a drunken person loses sense of the consequences of his actions, in the same manner, O my beloved, you exterminated their intoxication of alcohol, but you intoxicated them with faith to such magnitude that they offered sacrifices without concern for the consequences. As a matter of fact, the hypocrites used to comment that the believers sacrificed without realizing the consequences. They spent money for the sake of religion without worrying about their needs for tomorrow. They sacrificed their lives as if their only goal was to die, and not for war-booty or fame.

COUPLET 29

كَمْ مُحْدِثٍ مُسْتَنْطِقِ الْعِيْدَانِ
قَدْ صَارَ مِنْكَ مُحَدَّثَ الرَّحْمٰنِ

Many were addicted to playing music,
But you made them enjoy the bliss of converse with the Gracious God.

Many people used to play various musical instruments and would sing songs with lyrics, but by following the Holy Prophet[sa] the same people were able to communicate with the Ever-Loving God. It is reported in a *Ḥadīth* that the Holy Prophet[sa] said that in previous nations there were believers with whom God spoke and angels used to talk through their tongues. In my *ummah*, there would be people like this also. He presented Ḥaḍrat 'Umar bin Khaṭṭāb[ra] as an example of such individuals.[14]

COUPLET 30

كَمْ مُسْتَهَامٍ لِلرَّشُوْفِ تَعَشُّقًا
فَجَذَبْتَهُمْ جَذْبًا إِلَى الْفُرْقَانِ

Many were those who lusted for perfumed women,
But you made them adore the Book of God.

In the past people used to be madly in love with beautiful women, but O my beloved, you made them madly in love with the Word of God, the Holy Qur'ān, to such an extent that they confined themselves to the commandments of the Holy Qur'ān and lived their lives according to them. As such, the *Ḥadīth* refers to this world as a four-sided boundary for the believers.[15]

---

[14] *Ṣaḥīḥul-Bukhārī,* Kitābu Aḥādīthil-Anbiyā', Chapter 54, Ḥadīth no. 3469
[15] *Ṣaḥīḥul-Muslim,* Kitābuz-Zuhd, Bāb Ad-Dunyā Sijnul-Mu'min, Ḥadīth no. 7311

COUPLET 31

أَحْيَيْتَ أَمْوَاتَ الْقُرُوْنِ بِجَلْوَةٍ
مَاذَا يُمَاثِلُكَ بِهٰذَا الشَّانِ

With one look you resurrected to life the dead of ages;
Who can equal you in your glory?

This couplet mentions the superiority of the Holy Prophet[sa] over all of the other prophets, and this is proven by the fact that he was able to give spiritual life to his nation of Arabia in such a manner that no other prophet was able to do so. The most important and greatest mission of all prophets that came to this world was to spread the Unity of God. Allāh says in the Holy Qur'ān in *Sūrah an-Naḥl:*

وَلَقَدْ بَعَثْنَا فِيْ كُلِّ أُمَّةٍ رَّسُوْلًا أَنِ اعْبُدُوا اللّٰهَ وَاجْتَنِبُوا الطَّاغُوْتَ

And we did raise among every people a Messenger (preaching): 'worship Allāh and shun the Evil One'. (*an-Naḥl*, 16:37)

Keeping in mind the common mission of all prophets, we find that the followers of the Holy Prophet Muḥammad[sa] believed in the Oneness of God far more superior in quality as well as in depth when compared to other nations. Very few people from the nation of Noah[as] believed in him and the rest of his nation continued worshipping idols and carried on in their sinful activities. Eventually that nation was destroyed.

The condition of the nation of Moses[as] or the Israelites was such that in his lifetime when they saw another idol worshipping nation they said:

اجْعَلْ لَّنَآ اِلٰهًا كَمَا لَهُمْ اٰلِهَةٌ

Make for us a god just as this nation has gods other than Allāh. (*al-A'rāf*, 7:139)

When Moses[as] left them for a few days, they started worshipping a calf. In the same manner the followers of Jesus[as] after a very short time became involved in *shirk* and started to worship Jesus[as] himself. However, the spiritual powers of the Holy Prophet[sa] and his pure soul were able to give life to a people who were dead for centuries.

The world witnessed a remarkable revolution. The Arabian continent, which knew nothing other than idol worshipping, turned to the worship of One God within a short period of time. The Holy Prophet[sa] taught the lesson of Oneness of God to his followers in such a manner that they could never forget it. Day and night they continually proclaimed atop the minarets of their mosques, *"There is no one worthy of worship save Allāh."*

In essence, the life that was given to the nation of Arabia by the Holy Prophet Muḥammad[sa], the perfect one, has no match in any other nation or country. Ḥaḍrat Khalīfatul-Masīḥ II[ra] writes in *Tafsīr-e-Kabīr*:

> The Holy Prophet[sa] was sent to a nation which was in such a desolate state that it is difficult to find a similar condition in any

nation. But Allāh gave life to this nation through the advent of the Holy Prophet[sa] and made from them conquerors and rulers of the world. The interesting part is that most sick people have a desire to get better but the patients that were assigned to the Holy Prophet Muḥammad[sa] were not desirous of life. It seems that they wanted to be finished and their name be erased from the world. But the Holy Prophet[sa] cured that patient who wanted to die and considered it impossible to regain life. Not only did the patient survive but ended up giving life to thousands and thousands of other people in the world. The people of Mecca among whom the Holy Prophet[sa] lived, were average traders. They had no government or system of any kind. They did not have any respect or fame, but were living in darkness in a very lowly way of life. It is remarkable how these same people became full of life and spread all over the world. They arose just as an eagle pounces upon its prey and they destroyed the superpowers of their time. The Arabs had no respect and the low level government officials of the neighbouring countries used to order them around. However, after these people became slaves of the Holy Prophet[sa], they became so powerful that they would stand up to the greatest governments of that time. The governments of Caesar and Chosroes were destroyed when they clashed with them. Great kings presented themselves in their courts with their heads bowed and with their swords surrendered. This is an illustration of the revival that Allah the Exalted manifested upon the Holy Prophet[sa].

(*Tafsīr-e-Kabīr*, vol. 8, p. 398)

COUPLET 32

تَرَكُوا الْغَبُوقَ وَبَدَّلُوا مِنْ ذَوْقِهِ
ذَوْقَ الدُّعَاءِ بِلَيْلَةِ الْأَحْزَانِ

They abandoned the pleasures of the evening wine;
And embraced the joy of prayers in nights of grief

How wonderful was the revolution that took place amongst the Arabs. There was a time when they exhausted their nights in music, luxury, sports, eating and drinking, and now the same people were spending the dark hours of the night enjoying the pleasure of prayers and crying while prostrating to Allāh. This was a wonderful revolution that took place.

Pre-Islamic Arab customs include five different times when liquor was consumed and presented to guests within the day. There was a liquor named *jāshiriyyah* which was consumed before sunrise. The liquor called *ṣabūḥ* was consumed after sunrise. At noon-time it was *qail*. The one consumed in the afternoon was named *ghabūq*, and the drink for the evening was named *faḥmah*.[16] Islam changed these five times of drinking alcohol into the five daily prayers, and thus replaced each sinful activity with a good deed.

---

[16]*Lisānul-'Arab*, under the word Faḥmah

COUPLET 33

كَانُوْا بِرَنَّاتِ الْمَثَانِيْ قَبْلَهَا
قَدْ أُحْصِرُوْا فِيْ شَجِّهَا كَالْعَانِيْ

Earlier, they were bewitched by the charms of musical instruments;
They were held like captives who cannot move.

COUPLET 34

قَدْ كَانَ مَرْتَعُهُمْ أَغَانِيْ دَائِمًا
طَوْرًا بِغِيْدٍ تَارَةً بِدِنَانٍ

Their pleasure resorts were their music chambers;
At times they would flirt with women or indulge in heavy drinking.

COUPLET 35

مَا كَانَ فِكْرٌ غَيْرَ فِكْرِ غَوَانِيْ
أَوْ شُرْبِ رَاحٍ أَوْ خَيَالِ جِفَانٍ

They had no worry but the thought of pretty, singing women;
Or of wine and wine pots.

In the above three couplets there is another mention of those three sinful activities, which have been previously discussed.

COUPLET 36

كَانُوا كَمَشْغُوفِ الْفَسَادِ بِجَهْلِهِمْ
رَاضِيْنَ بِالْأَوْسَاخِ وَ الْأَدْرَانِ

They were eager to violate peace and order due to their ignorance;
And were quite pleased to live in dirt and filth.

COUPLET 37

عَيْبَانِ كَانَ شِعَارَهُمْ مِنْ جَهْلِهِمْ
حُمْقُ الْحِمَارِ وَ وَثْبَةُ السِّرْحَانِ

Due to ignorance, two were the major faults they were known by:
the obstinacy of a donkey and the ferocity of the wolf.

In the last two couplets there is mention of the ills of the Arabian civilization. The famous poet Maulānā Alṭāf Ḥusain Ḥālī states their condition in his poetry as follows:

They acted just as beasts and were known for their robbing and looting. They spent their life in fighting and creating trouble and had no justice among them. They were so keen on killing that they can only be compared to the beasts of the jungle. They were stubborn and once they started a fight there was no way to stop it. If only two people had an argument, hundreds would become involved. If there was only one small little spark the country would make a fire out of it. As an example of this, there was a fight between Bakr and Taghlab[17] which lasted almost fifty years. This fight spread throughout Arabia and many tribes were completely annihilated. It was not a fight over land or government, but only a manifestation of their ignorance. They would fight over who was allowed to graze their pastures or whose horse should be first or who would receive water first. Over their petty issues they fought and drew their swords. Day and night they were engrossed in gambling, and drinking became engraved in their very nature. They were living a life of luxury and carelessness, and basically, had lost their senses. Their condition was the worst in every respect. Centuries had passed in such a state and their sins had overshadowed their virtues.[18]

---

[17]Bakr and Taghlab are the names of two Arab tribes that were battling each other. Their main battle was named the Battle of Basūs. There was a woman from the family of Bakr whose name was Basūs. Bakr had a guest whose camel strayed into the land of Kulaib, while grazing. Kulaib belonged to the family of Taghlab. So Kulaib shot an arrow at its utter. The Bakr tribe became angry over this and a person named Muhalhil killed Kulaib with a dagger. This started a battle among the tribes, which continued for a long time.

[18]*Musaddas Madd-o-Jazar Islām,* Musaddas Hālī Shamsul-'Ulamā', p. 14–15, Feroz Sons Lahore, First Edition (1988)

COUPLETS 38 and 39

فَطَلَعْتَ يَا شَمْسَ الْهُدٰى نُصْحًا لَّهُمْ
لِتُضِيْئَهُمْ مِنْ وَّجْهِكَ النُّوْرَانِيْ

It was then O sun of guidance that you arose on the horizon,
To give them light and benevolence with your lustrous face.

أُرْسِلْتَ مِنْ رَّبٍّ كَرِيْمٍ مُّحْسِنٍ
فِي الْفِتْنَةِ الصَّمَّاءِ وَ الطُّغْيَانِ

You were sent by your Lord, the Noble, the Beneficent,
At a time when evil and vice deluged.

In these two couplets there is a reference to that great revolution that took place during the advent of the Holy Prophet[sa], in a nation that was stubborn, ignorant and was the shame of humanity. At this point it is appropriate to quote the address of Ḥaḍrat Ja'far bin Abī Ṭālib which he delivered in front of the king of Abyssinia when the Quraish demanded the return of the Muslim refugees. Ḥaḍrat Ja'far said in a very emotional manner:

> Your Majesty, our condition was such that we were at the lowest level of ignorance. We used to worship idols. Our language was filthy. We used to eat dead animals. We had no quality of humanity within us. Then Allāh, Who is Gracious to the whole

world sent Muḥammad, may peace and blessings of Allāh be upon him, to us as a messenger. We are fully aware of the respectable family he comes from, his truthfulness, his pure way of life, and his honesty. As Allāh had desired, he brought to us a message from Allāh that we should only believe in one God, we should not setup equals with Him or His Qualities, and we should not worship idols. We should always speak the truth and we should always deal honestly. We should have sympathy for all other creatures and guard the rights of our neighbours, respect labourers, not devour the property of orphans and live a life which should be clean and righteous, pray to God, forget about food and drink for Him and spend on the poor for the sake of God.

O King ... upon us believing these things we were tortured to an extent that we ... had to leave our country and live ... in poverty. We cannot find any room in our country to live and I am sure that your justice and kindness will not let you harm us poor people.

(*Sawāneḥ 'Umrī Ḥaḍrat Muḥammad*[sa] *Ṣāḥib Bānī-e-Islām,* Shardhiay Parkāsh Dev Jī, p. 37–38, Publisher Narā'in Datt Sehgal and Sons, Lahore, 10th edition)

In the above address Ḥaḍrat Ja'far has briefly described the condition of the Arabian nation before the advent of Islam and the Islamic teachings which brought about a revolution. Allāh has mentioned this great revolution among the Arabian nation in Sūrah al-Furqān in its last *rukū'*.

وَعِبَادُ الرَّحْمٰنِ الَّذِيْنَ يَمْشُوْنَ عَلَى الْاَرْضِ هَوْنًا وَّ اِذَا خَاطَبَهُمُ الْجٰهِلُوْنَ قَالُوْا سَلٰمًا

> **And the servants of the Gracious God are those who walk on the earth in a dignified manner and when the ignorant address them they say 'Peace'.** (*al-Furqān*, 25:64)

This means that a change has taken place among the people whom Allāh has prepared by His Grace and through His prophet. Dignity and humility has taken the place of the arrogant way of living. They used to be proud to walk in an arrogant manner under the influence of alcohol as the poet Qais bin Khaṭīm states:

اذا ما اصطبحت اربعا خطّ میزری

When I drink four glasses of liquor in the morning
then I walk with arrogance and my drawstring draws
a line on the ground as I walk.

(*Tashīlud-Dirāsah Fī Sharḥil-Ḥimāsah,* Bābul-Ḥimāsah, Wa Qāla Qais bin Khaṭīm, p. 44, translated by Maulawī Dhul-Fiqār 'Alī, Published by 'Abdut-Tawwāb Academy, Multan, March 1986)

And now their condition is such that they walk with dignity and self restrain. They have no arrogance left in them and they present themselves to others with kindness and with etiquette. Before the advent of Islam, they used to be proud of ignorance, i.e., fighting, as the poet 'Amr bin Kulthūm Taghlabī wrote:

الالايجهلن احد علينا

فنجهل فوق جهل الجاهلينا

Beware nobody should try ignorance with us (meaning do not start fights with us)
Otherwise we would show you we are more ignorant than you.

(*Sharḥul-Mu'allaqātil-'Ashri,* Mu'allaqah 'Amr bin Kulthūm, p. 121, Dāru Iḥyā'it-Turāthil-'Arabiyy)

However, the people of God after the acceptance of Islam respond with the word *peace or Salām* when they are encountered by the ignorant as it is quoted in Sūrah al-Furqān:

وَّ اِذَا خَاطَبَهُمُ الْجٰهِلُوْنَ قَالُوْا سَلٰمًا

Meaning, When these people are addressed by the ignorant meaning those who want to fight, they respond with peace. (*al-Furqān,* 25:64)

In other words, they say that we are desirous of peace and tranquillity and we do not want any trouble.

During the era of ignorance, people used to spend their time in drinking, gambling, womanizing, dancing, music and playing around. Now, not only have they left these bad habits, but يَبِيْتُوْنَ لِرَبِّهِمْ سُجَّدًا وَّ قِيَامًا (al-Furqān 25:65) they spend their nights in the worship of God and offering prayers and prostrating.

In another place the Holy Qur'ān says:

تَتَجَافَىٰ جُنُوبُهُمْ عَنِ الْمَضَاجِعِ يَدْعُونَ رَبَّهُمْ خَوْفًا وَطَمَعًا ۔

Their sides keep away from their beds; and they call on their Lord in fear and hope. (*as-Sajdah,* 32:17)

In the days of ignorance they had no concept of the Day of Judgment. Their motto was to eat, drink and be merry because death awaits its day. Therefore, they had no concept of sin being something to be accounted for. After accepting Islam they started praying to their Lord:

رَبَّنَا اصْرِفْ عَنَّا عَذَابَ جَهَنَّمَ

Meaning, O our Lord, protect us from the punishment of Hell. (*al-Furqān,* 25:66)

In other words, they were concerned about the Day of Judgment constantly.

In the days of ignorance they used to throw away their money in pursuit of their customs, music, fame, luxury, or gambling. They would not find it within their hearts to spend any money for the poor, needy, widows or orphans. These were the same people who after accepting Islam have been described in the Holy Qur'ān as:

لَمْ يُسْرِفُوا وَلَمْ يَقْتُرُوا

Neither stingy, nor exuberant. (*al-Furqān,* 25:68)

In other words, now they have balanced the spending of their money in both of these conditions.

In the times of ignorance, the whole of Arabia was engulfed in idol worshipping, intoxication, cheating, killing and looting. Idol worship was so prevalent that every tribe had its own idol. There were 360 idols inside the *Ka'bah*. The Quraish considered idol worship a matter of life and death. The Holy Qur'ān states that these people would say:

إِنْ نَّتَّبِعِ الْهُدٰى مَعَكَ نُتَخَطَّفْ مِنْ اَرْضِنَا

If we accept Islam and give up idol worship then we have no place of protection on this earth. (*al-Qaṣaṣ*, 28:58)

However, idol worshipping was removed from the land of Arabia in such a manner that for 1,400 years it has not been able to return. The concept of Oneness of God became so firmly established in their blood that they accepted and embraced all types of tortures and cruelties for the sake of their religion. The non-believers at one time arrested Ḥaḍrat Khubaib[ra]. When the time came for his execution and he laid his head in front of the executioner, he recited the following two couplets before the sword fell upon him:

ولستُ أبالی حینَ أقتلُ مُسلمًا

علی أیّ جنب کانَ لِلّٰہِ مَصرعی

وذٰلکَ فی ذاتِ الإلٰہِ وإن یّشاء

يُبَارِكْ عَلٰى أَوْصَالِ شِلْوٍ مُمَزَّعِ

Since I am being killed in the condition of being a Muslim, I am not concerned that in the cause of Allāh, how my body falls. My dying is for the sake of Allāh, and if He so wishes He shall bless every part of my body.

(*Ṣaḥīḥul-Bukhārī,* Kitābul-Maghāzī, Chapter 10/10, Ḥadīth no. 3989)

As soon as Ḥaḍrat Khubaib[ra] recited the last couplet, the sword fell upon his neck and his head separated from his body. It was a very dreadful and moving scene. Among the people who had gathered to witness this event was Sa'īd bin 'Āmir, who later converted to Islam. Whenever the mention of the murder of Ḥaḍrat Khubaib[ra] ever came up in any discussion he used to faint.[19] The murderers of Ḥaḍrat Khubaib[ra] have been long forgotten and there is no mention of them but the name of Ḥaḍrat Khubaib[ra] lives forever.

کشتگانِ خنجرِ تسلیم را
ہر زماں از غیب جانِ دیگر است

The one who is killed by the sword of faithfulness,
They have been given a new life and it has been proven in every age (i.e. throughout history).

(*Siyarul-Auliyā',* Syed Muḥammad Mubarak 'Alawī Karmanawī, translated by I'jāzul-Ḥaqq Qudsī, Fourth Point Ḥaḍrat Sheikh Quṭb-ud-Dīn Bakhtiyār Raḥmatullāh 'Alaih...)

---

[19] *Usdul-Ghābah Fī Ma'rifatiṣ-Ṣaḥābah,* vol. 2, p. 259, Sa'd bin 'Āmir, Dārul-Fikr, Beirut, edn. 2003

In the era of ignorance there were looters and robbers. Over minor issues battles would start and continue for months and years. However, after accepting Islam, their condition has been described in the Holy Qur'ān as such:

وَلَا تَقْتُلُوا النَّفْسَ الَّتِي حَرَّمَ اللَّهُ إِلَّا بِالْحَقِّ

They do not murder anyone whose murder has not been made lawful by the Shariah. (*al-Furqān*, 25:69)

They used to boast and were proud of adultery and womanizing; however, after accepting Islam, they gave up these habits.

Murthad al-Ghanawī was a strong young man. He would liberate the Muslim prisoners from Mecca and take them to Medina. One time he called for a prisoner and upon hearing his voice one of the prostitutes of Mecca named 'Unāq who had been friends with Murthad in the past came around. She greeted him and insisted he should spend the night with her. Murthad answered her, 'O 'Unāq, the Prophet of Allāh has outlawed adultery for us.'

When she realized that Murthad was persistent on his refusal, she raised her voice announcing that this is the person who steals your prisoners. Murthad ran and hid in a cave of the hills of Khanzamah. Eight people went to search for him and they came close to him. Some of them relieved themselves there and some of the urine fell upon him, but they could not see him and they returned. Afterwards, Murthad went back to fetch a prisoner and brought him back to Medina.[20]

This incident is a great illustration of the transformation that had taken place. A prostitute who was his close friend before the advent of Islam was calling him to spend a night with her and he refused knowing that his life would be in danger, and his only response was that the Prophet had outlawed adultery and therefore I cannot do it.

Allāh also describes in the Holy Qur'ān:

وَالَّذِينَ لَا يَشْهَدُونَ الزُّورَ وَإِذَا مَرُّوا بِاللَّغْوِ مَرُّوا كِرَامًا

And those who bear not false witness, and when they pass by anything vain, they pass on with dignity. (*al-Furqān*, 25:73)

This verse means that the people whose former condition did not distinguish lies from truth, now do not give any false witness nor do they make any false agreements and when they see people engaged in absurd and foolish activities, they refrain from involving themselves.

The Holy Qur'ān says:

وَالَّذِينَ إِذَا ذُكِّرُوا بِآيَاتِ رَبِّهِمْ لَمْ يَخِرُّوا عَلَيْهَا صُمًّا وَعُمْيَانًا

That these same people who would not listen to the truth nor try to comprehend it, now when the Words of Allāh

[20] *Sunan An-Nasa'ī*, Kitābun-Nikāḥ, Bābu Tazwījiz-Zāniyah, Ḥadīth no. 3228

are recited to them, they act on them with contemplation and not as blind and deaf people. (*al-Furqān*, 25:74)

In the days of ignorance they were living an unclean life. Spirituality did not exist among them. Now they live in such cleanliness, spirituality and righteousness, that they keep on praying in the following words:

رَبَّنَا هَبْ لَنَا مِنْ اَزْوَاجِنَا وَ ذُرِّيّٰتِنَا قُرَّةَ اَعْيُنٍ وَّ اجْعَلْنَا لِلْمُتَّقِيْنَ اِمَامًا

O our Lord, mould our wives and our children in spirituality that they become the delight of our eyes and make us the leaders of the righteous. (*al-Furqān*, 25:75)

This verse explains that their righteousness and spirituality had advanced to such a level that now they cannot tolerate associating with someone who is not righteous. They now desire from Allāh that their friends, relatives, and associates should be righteous and clean.

This revolution changed the scope, the methods, and angles of their contemplation and thinking. The abilities within them that had died for centuries came to life and became the basis for reviving the world. The Promised Messiah[as] has explained this unprecedented revolution in his Urdu poetry:

کہتے ہیں یورپ کے ناداں یہ نبیؐ کامل نہیں
وحشیوں میں دیں کو پھیلانا یہ کیا مشکل تھا کار

پر بنانا آدمی وحشی کو ہے اک معجزہ
معنئ رازِ نبوت ہے اِسی سے آشکار
نور لائے آسماں سے خود بھی وہ اک نور تھے
قوم وحشی میں اگر پیدا ہوئے کیا جائے عار
روشنی میں مہر تاباں کی بھلا کیا فرق ہو
گرچہ نکلے روم کی سرحد سے یا از زنگبار

The ignorant people of Europe say the Holy Prophet[sa] is not a perfect being,
And it was not a big accomplishment to spread religion among wild-natured people.

The fact is that it is a miracle to change a beast into a human being.
In this fact, is the secret of prophethood.

He brought light from heaven and he was a light himself.
So what if he was raised among a nation of beasts? The light of the sun is indifferent whether it rises in Rome or Zanzibar.

(*Barāhīn-e-Aḥmadiyya*, part 4, *Rūḥānī Khazā'in*, vol. 1, p. 144)

COUPLET 40

يَا لَلْفَتٰى مَا حُسْنُهٗ وَ جَمَالُهٗ
رَيَّاهُ يُصْبِى الْقَلْبَ كَا لرَّيْحَانِ

What a noble man! What a man of glory!
His breath smells like the fragrance of sweet basil.

COUPLET 41

وَجْهُ الْمُهَيْمِنِ ظَاهِرٌ فِىْ وَجْهِهٖ
وَ شُئُوْنُهٗ لَمَعَتْ بِهٰذَا الشَّاْنِ

The Protector (God) is visible in his face;
And all of his virtues shine in great glory.

The first part of the couplet could mean that in the pleasure of the Holy Prophet[sa] was a reflection of the pleasure of Allāh and that his person is a manifestation of God Himself, and that this manifestation has reflected itself in all of his great works.

This couplet mentions another superiority of the Holy Prophet[sa] over other prophets. It says that the person of the Holy Prophet[sa] was a complete and perfect manifestation of God Himself. The previous prophets and other pious people became manifestations of Allāh according to their capacities or spiritual levels, but none from among them was able to become a perfect manifestation. The perfect manifestation was only the Holy Prophet[sa].

In Sūrah Fātiḥah, there are four great attributes of Allāh that have been mentioned. They are: *Mālikiyyat* (Masterhood), *Raḥīmiyyat* (Mercifulness,) *Raḥmāniyyat* (Benevolence), and *Rabbul-'Ālāmīn* (Lord of all the worlds).

It is very obvious that all the prophets that appeared before the Holy Prophet[sa] were sent to a particular nation or geographical area. They became a reflection of the four attributes of Allāh, but only in a partial way. For example, they were a reflection of the attribute *Rabūbiyyat*, meaning Lordship, but could not be a reflection of the attribute *Rabbul-'Ālamīn*, Lord of all the worlds, because they were not sent to all the nations. The time of their prophethood was limited as well. On the other hand, the Holy Prophet[sa] was sent to all nations and for all times to come. Therefore, he became a perfect manifestation of the attribute *Rabbul-'Ālamīn*.

The same is the situation with the remaining three attributes. For example, under the attribute of *Raḥmāniyyat*, Allāh has created the sun, moon, wind, earth, etc., which provide benefit to all people whether they are believers or disbelievers. In the same manner the Holy Prophet[sa] unlike the previous prophets was sent for the whole world and his light, just like the light of the sun, was not restrained to a particular nation and his benefits have not been limited to any area or timeframe in any respect. His blessings are for all people in general and for all times to come, and will never be discontinued. His blessings are available to the People of the Book as well as to the people who were not given a book. But the prophets who appeared before him could not be the perfect manifestation of this attribute of Allāh.

It is established that Jesus[as] only addressed himself to the Children of Israel and stated clearly that he had not been sent but unto the lost sheep of the house of Israel.[21] As a matter of fact, he referred to the other nationalities that were present in Palestine at that time as swine and dogs, and did not preach to them.

Similarly Moses[as] limited his circle of propagation to the Children of Israel. However, the Holy Prophet[sa] propagated to every nation and people of every country. He sent invitations and letters of propagation to the Caesar of Rome, Chosroes, King of Egypt, and to the kings of many other countries because Allāh had given him that glory as is explained by this Persian couplet:

آفتابِ ہر زمین و ہر زماں
رہبرِ ہر اسود و ہر احمرے

He is the sun for all lands and all times,
And he is the guide of all people whether they are black or red.

(*Barāhīn-e-Aḥmadiyya,* Part I, *Rūḥānī Khazā'in,* vol. 1, p. 19)

So it is clear that the Holy Prophet[sa] was the one who was the perfect manifestation of God Himself. The Promised Messiah[as] writes in his Persian poetry:

---

[21] Matthew 15:24

زاں نمط شد محو دلبر کز کمالِ اتحاد
پیکرِ او شد سراسر صورتِ ربِّ رحیم
بُوئے محبوبِ حقیقی میدمد زاں رُوئے پاک
ذاتِ حقانی صفاتش مظہر ذاتِ قدیم

This means that Prophet Muḥammad[sa] became absorbed in his beloved Allāh to such a degree that through this union, which was perfect, he became a reflection of Allāh Himself. We can smell the fine fragrance of our beloved Allāh from the face of the Holy Prophet[sa]. His personality, by reflecting divine attributes, became a perfect reflection of the Ever-Living God.

(*Tauḍīḥ-e-Marām, Rūḥānī Khazā'in*, vol. 3, p. 62)

COUPLET 42

فَلِذَا يُحَبُّ وَ يُسْتَحَقُّ جَمَالُهٗ
شَغَفًا بِهٖ مِنْ زُمْرَةِ الْاَخْدَانِ

That is why he is beloved. Indeed his beautiful virtues demand;
That he be adored to the exclusion of all.

The writer of the Qaṣīdah asks the interesting question, 'since my beloved Muḥammad[sa] is a perfect manifestation of Allāh, then why would I leave him and make someone else my beloved?'

There is a story of a man who decided to get a second wife. His first wife petitioned to the court that he should not be allowed to marry another woman. On the court date, the first wife was brought in to plead her case. She removed her veil and said that when he has such a beautiful wife, he should not be allowed to get another wife. A Sufi saint, who was present in that court room, fainted upon hearing that. Someone from the audience remarked that now people would come to know what kind of a Sufi he really was – as he had become overwhelmed with one look at a beautiful woman. When the Sufi regained consciousness, he explained that actually he saw the manifestation of Allāh's beauty in the beauty of that woman. When a beautiful woman is so proud of her beauty that she is not willing to take in a competitor, then how can Allāh, Who is the Most Beautiful Being and the Source of beauty, allow someone to be equal to Him?

So the Promised Messiah[as] here states that when his beloved Muḥammad[sa] is more beautiful, handsome and attractive than all mankind, then why not relinquish everyone else and just fall in love with him?

COUPLET 43

سُجُحٌ كَرِيْمٌ بَاذِلٌ خِلُّ التُّقٰى
خِرْقٌ وَّ فَاقَ طَوَائِفَ الْفِتْيَانِ

Of noble character, revered, bounteous, friend of the God-fearing;

He excels all in the field of virtue.

This couplet mentions a few other virtues of the Holy Prophet[sa]. Allāh says in the Holy Qur'ān in praise of the Holy Prophet[sa]:

اِنَّكَ لَعَلٰى خُلُقٍ عَظِيْمٍ

You do surely possess high moral excellences. (*al-Qalam*, 68:5)

COUPLET 44

فَاقَ الْوَرٰى بِكَمَالِهٖ وَ جَمَالِهٖ
وَ جَلَالِهٖ وَجَنَانِهِ الرَّيَّانٖ

In excellence and beauty, he surpasses all;
And in glory and cheerfulness of heart.

This couplet means that in the qualities mentioned, there is no one who can match the Holy Prophet[sa]. His grandeur was of a kind that even emperors and kings were afraid of him. The Holy Prophet[sa] said that even those governments that were at a distance of two months travel from him were in awe of him.[22] In *Ṣaḥiḥ Bukhārī* it is mentioned that when the Caesar of Rome received the letter sent

[22] *Kitābus-Sunanil-Kubrā Lil-Baihaqī*, vol. 2, p. 572, Jimā'u Abwābiṣ-Ṣalāti Bin-Najāsati..., Bābu Ainama Adrakatkaṣ-Ṣalātu, Ḥadīth no. 4368, Maktabatur-Rushdi, Beirut (2004)

by the Holy Prophet[sa], he had called Abū Sufyān to obtain some information from him. Abū Sufyān immediately stated:

لَقَدْ أَمِرَ أَمْرُ ابْنِ أَبِي كَبْشَةَ أَنَّهُ يَخَافُهُ مَلِكُ بَنِي الصفر

> The matter of this person (i.e. Muḥammad[sa]) has reached such a level that even the King of Rome is afraid of him.
> (*Ṣaḥīḥul-Bukhārī,* Kitābul-Bad'il-Waḥyi, ch.6, Ḥadīth no. 7)

Similarly, an individual who came to the Holy Prophet[sa] was so awe-inspired that he started trembling. The Holy Prophet[sa] said, 'Do not be frightened of me. I am the son of a woman who used to eat dried meat.'

In the above two couplets, the Promised Messiah[as] has summarized the top attributes and qualities of the Holy Prophet[sa]. Similarly in his Arabic poetry he writes:

وفی مهجتی فور وجیش لامدحا

سلالة انوار الكريم محمدًا

كريم السجايا اكمل العلم و النّهى

شفيع البرايا منبع الفضل و الهدیٰ

تبصر خصيمي هل ترىٰ من مشاكة

بتلك الصفات الصالحات باحمدا

بشير نذير آمر مانع معًا

حکیم بحکمة الجلیلة یقتدی

In my heart I have so much passion and emotion that I should praise the Holy Prophet[sa], who is the essence of the attributes of Allāh. He has high morals and is perfect in his knowledge and intelligence. He is the one who intercedes on behalf of other creatures and is the fountain of blessings and guidance. Tell me, is there another person who has similar qualities as Aḥmad? At the same time he is the one announcing good news and being a warner. He is the one who orders you to do good and forbids you to do evil. He is full of wisdom, and through the light of his wisdom he became the leader of the world.

(*Karāmātuṣ-Ṣādiqīn, Rūḥānī Khazā'in*, vol. 7, p. 91)

In the last couplet there is a beautiful description of all the qualities that should be in a perfect guide and a holy prophet who brings a law.

COUPLET 45

لَا شَكَّ أَنَّ مُحَمَّدًا خَيْرُ الْوَرٰى
رِيْقُ الْكِرَامِ وَ نُخْبَةُ الْأَعْيَانِ

Without any doubt, Muḥammad[sa] is the best of the best—

a man of extreme generosity, the soul and strength of the nobles, the elect among the elite.

COUPLET 46

تَمَّتْ عَلَيْهِ صِفَاتُ كُلِّ مَزِيَّةٍ
خُتِمَتْ بِهٖ نَعْمَآءُ كُلِّ زَمَانٖ

All noble virtues culminated in his person,
The blessings of all times reached their apex in him.

Volumes of books can be written to explain this couplet. The writer of the Qaṣīdah has miraculously and wonderfully encapsulated the qualities of the Holy Prophet[sa] in a few words. He states that the qualities and the wonders by which a person becomes distinguished over others were present in the personality of the Holy Prophet[sa] in their perfect form and the blessings of all ages were bestowed upon him in a perfect manner.

In the first part of the couplet it was stated that the Holy Prophet[sa] is the perfect being from among the whole of mankind, and as a human being, all the qualities that could ever be present in any one person were found in his personality. This is another way of expressing the subject that is mentioned in the *Ḥadīth-e-Qudsī*:

لولاک لما خلقتُ الافلاک

We would not have created the universe if We had not created you.

(*Silsilatul-Aḥādīthiḍ-Ḍaʿīfati Wal-Mauḍūʿāti*, vol. 1, by Muḥammad Nāṣir-ud-Dīn Al-Bāni, p. 450, Ḥadīth no. 282, Maktabatul-Maʿārifi, Riyad, 2000 A.D.)

In this *ḥadīth* the Holy Prophet[sa] has been described as the central point of the circle of humanity. In other words, he was the perfect human being.

In 1928, when I was residing in a hotel in Haifa, Palestine, I was sitting on the balcony on the second floor when two businessmen from Nablis, who were also staying in the hotel, came and started a conversation with me. During our conversation they asked regarding this *ḥadīth*. I gave them a general description but it did not satisfy them. One of them said that it seems illogical that if one person was not to be created, then the whole world would not have been created.

I felt a disturbance in my heart because of his objection and I had a great desire at that moment to find a solution that would satisfy him. *Alḥamdulillāh*, all of a sudden this matter was clarified in my heart which I proceeded to explain to them. I said that when a person starts to build something it is normally his desire to make it so perfect that it will have no shortcomings so he tries his best in order to achieve that. The reason for the defects in the works of human beings is that they do not have perfect knowledge nor do they have control over everything.

For example, a watchmaker, no matter how professional he is in his trade, would not be able to build a watch that would continue to run forever without any defects. Why can he not make such a watch? It is because he does not have perfect knowledge or the control to create such materials that would last forever and never became defective. So the defects in the works of human beings are a direct result of these two things: lack of perfect knowledge and lack of control over creation. However, Allāh has perfect knowledge and perfect control. So once He decides to make something, no defect can appear in it. In this *ḥadīth* it is described that Allāh says that O Muḥammad[sa], when I began the process of creating human beings and I ordained them to be better than all other beings, it was essential that I create such a human being who was perfect in all qualities that could manifest within human beings; and that perfect being is you. Therefore, if I had not envisioned creating you then I would not have started the process of creation, and once I started it, then I had to make you, the perfect human being. Upon hearing this, the businessmen were pleased and admitted that they really understood the meaning of this *ḥadīth* for the first time.

The Promised Messiah[as] wrote:

> Among the good qualities of human beings is to show excellent manners. About the Holy Prophet[sa], Allāh has stated in the Holy Qur'ān that O prophet you possess high moral excellences.
>
> إِنَّكَ لَعَلٰى خُلُقٍ عَظِيمٍ
>
> (*al-Qalam 68:5*)
>
> Meaning that all of the best manners were present in the personality of the Holy Prophet[sa] and any better manners could

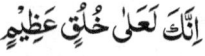

not be imagined because the word 'Aẓīm used here is only used in Arabic when something is used in its perfect form.

(*Barāhīn-e-Aḥmadiyya*, part 4, *Rūḥānī Khazā'in*, vol. 1, p. 194, footnote no. 11)

One of the excellent qualities is to forgive someone when you have the power to punish them. This quality was reflected in the Holy Prophet[sa] in such a manner that there is no comparison to it.

One time the Holy Prophet[sa] was returning from a battle. It was noon time and the Muslim army was resting. The Holy Prophet[sa] went to the side by himself and lay under a tree to relax. The companions who were with him also found places where they could relax. The Holy Prophet[sa] was alone when suddenly an enemy named Da'thūr got close to him and took hold of his sword which was hanging on the tree. Meanwhile the Holy Prophet[sa] woke up. Da'thūr said, *O Muḥammad, tell me who can save you from me now?*

In this perilous situation, even the bravest of the brave lose their senses, but the Prophet's bravery and trust in God was of such magnitude that he replied, *Allāh.* This word, Allāh, was uttered by the Holy Prophet[sa] with such conviction and authority that the man's heart trembled and his body shook and the sword fell out of his hand. Then the Holy Prophet[sa] picked up the sword and asked him who could save him now. He asked for mercy and the Prophet forgave a man who was about to take his life.[23] This is an excellent example of the quality of forgiveness.

---

[23] *As-Sīratul-Ḥalabiyyah,* 'Allāmah Abil-Faraj Nūrid-Dīn, vol. 2, p. 290, Bābu Dhikri Maghāzīhī (Ghazwatu Dhī 'Amrin), Dārul-Kutubil-'Ilmiyyah, Beirut (2002)

On the day of the victory of Mecca, the enemies were presented to the Holy Prophet[sa], who for 13 years, inflicted inhumane cruelties upon him and his followers. These enemies had boycotted him for three years, seized properties of the Muslims, looted their wealth and expelled them out of their homes. Now the Muslims were in a position where they were in control and the slightest gesture from the Holy Prophet[sa] would have been enough for all of them to be killed. However, he did not say any harsh words to them. On the other hand, he asked them, 'Tell me, how shall I treat you?'

With humility and shame, and with their heads lowered, they answered that they expect the same treatment from the Holy Prophet[sa] as that of Prophet Joseph[as] towards his brothers. Upon hearing this answer, and disregarding all of their previous cruelties and atrocities, he said, 'Go ahead, there is no blame on you. May Allāh forgive you, and certainly He is the Best in showing mercy. Go, you are all free to go.'[24]

It is described in a *Ḥadīth* that when these people left the *Ka'bah*, they left as if they were walking from out of their graves and all of them embraced Islam.[25] Among other conquerors there is not a single example of similar forgiveness.

In the same manner, it is an excellent quality of manners when a person treats his enemy nicely, prays for him instead of cursing him,

---

[24] *Subulul-Hudā War-Rashād,* Imām Muḥammad bin Yūsuf, vol. 5, p. 242, Al-Bābus-Sābi'u Wal-'Ishrūna Fī Ghazwātil-Fatḥil-A'ẓam...Dhikru Khuṭbati Yaumil-Fatḥi, Dārul-Kutubil-'Ilmiyyah, Beirut (1993)

[25] *Kitābus-Sunanil-Kubrā Lil-Baihaqī,* vol. 9, p. 195, Jimā'u Abwābis-Siyar, Bābu Fatḥi Makkata Ḥarrasahallāhu Ta'āla, Ḥadīth no. 4368, Maktabatur-Rushdi, Beirut (2004)

and does favours upon him and exhibits benevolence in response to his evil actions.

In London, from 1945 to the early part of 1946, for about a year, I used to debate in Hyde Park every Friday, with a Christian named Mr. Green. He believed according to his calculation from the Bible that Jesus Christ was going to descend in 1954. He had published many articles on this issue. The terms of the debate were agreed upon that the first Friday he would state his objections against the Holy Prophet[sa] and the Holy Qur'ān, and I would respond. On the next Friday, I would state my objections against Christianity and he would respond. The debates lasted for about three hours, and speeches used to be about ten minutes each, and the audience was given permission to ask questions. By the Grace of Allāh, these debates were very successful and eventually Mr. Green accepted his defeat and gave up on the debates.

One time he was trying to establish that Jesus Christ had better manners and morals than the Holy Prophet[sa]. He cited the incident that when Jesus was on the cross he prayed for the Jews, his enemies, in the following words: 'O Father, forgive them for they know not what they do.'[26] In other words, they are treating me in this manner because they lack knowledge. Mr. Green stated that this type of morality was not displayed by any other prophet including the Holy Prophet Muḥammad[sa].

I responded to him by saying that we believe in Jesus[as] as being a prophet and as a person who possessed excellent morals. However, it is a mistake to state that no one is equal to him in good morals. Mr. Green's statement about the Holy Prophet[sa] shows that he has

[26] Luke 23:34

no knowledge of the history of Islam. The Holy Prophet[sa] was also injured by the stones thrown at him by his enemies at the Battle of Uḥud and fell unconscious. The non-believers started announcing that Muḥammad[sa] had been killed.[27] When the Holy Prophet[sa] regained consciousness he was cleaning the blood from his wounds and kept on praying, 'O my Allāh, guide my people because they do not know.'[28] In other words, they are mistreating me because of their lack of knowledge.

The prayers of both of these prophets seem to be the same on the surface. It seems that both of them desired not to hurt their enemies. However, there is a big difference between the two. The prayer of Jesus Christ was about the Jews who had put him on the cross, that they be forgiven. However the prayer of the Holy Prophet[sa] about the people who had injured him was not only that they be forgiven, but that they be guided, i.e., he wanted Allāh to give them the same blessings that he received himself. This prayer of the Holy Prophet[sa] has such superiority over the prayer of Jesus Christ that it is amazing. The prayer of the Holy Prophet[sa] becomes even clearer when we see the results of these prayers.

From the Gospels it can be established that the punishment for the Jews that Jesus[as] described was that the Kingdom of Heaven would be taken away from them, and in fact, it was taken away from them. Now, how does this establish that the prayer of Jesus[as] was accepted and the Jews were forgiven? On the contrary, it seems

---

[27] *Subulul-Hudā War-Rashād,* Imām Muḥammad bin Yūsuf, vol. 4, p. 248, Al-Bābuth-Thālith Fī Ghazwātil-Uḥud, Dārul-Kutubil-'Ilmiyyah, Beirut (1993)

[28] *Ash-Shifā'u Bi-Ta'rīfi Ḥuqūqil-Muṣṭafā,* Qāḍī 'Ayyād, vol. 1, p. 72–73, Faṣl Wa Ammal-Ḥilmu, Dārul-Kutubil-'Ilmiyyah, Beirut (2002)

that the prayer of Jesus[as] at this difficult time was not accepted and the Jews were not forgiven, because if they were forgiven then the Kingdom of Heaven would not have been taken from them. Since it is obvious the Kingdom of Heaven was taken away from them, we have no choice but to acknowledge that the prayer to forgive the Jews was not accepted.

However, the prayer of the Holy Prophet[sa] that Allāh may provide guidance to his people was accepted. The glory of the acceptance of this prayer was manifested on the day of the victory of Mecca in a manner no one in the world can deny. When the Holy Prophet[sa] forgave all of his enemies on the day of victory, they all accepted Islam. By receiving this guidance they became a proof of the acceptance of the prayers of the Holy Prophet[sa] that Allāh provide them guidance. By the Grace of Allāh, the Holy Prophet[sa] was not only unique in his qualities of forgiveness and in his treatment of others, but in all other qualities such as bravery, self respect, charity, truthfulness, doing favours, sacrifices, faithfulness, steadfastness, patience, trust in Allāh, and kindness and affection towards the creatures of Allāh.

Anyone who desires to study the details of how the moral qualities of the Holy Prophet[sa] were better than other prophets should study the commentary of Sūrah al-Kauthar written by Khalīfatul-Masīḥ II, Ḥaḍrat Mirzā Bashīr-ud-Dīn Maḥmūd Aḥmad, in his *Tafsīr-e-Kabīr* [the Large Commentary].

The second part of this couplet describes that blessings have been perfected by the Holy Prophet[sa] for all times to come. In the Holy Qur'ān, blessings have been described in worldly matters as *'kingdom'* and in the spiritual world as *'prophethood.'* It is unparalleled how the Holy Prophet[sa] was given kingdom in the worldly sense and how his people were faithful and ready to sacrifice their lives for him. In his lifetime, Allāh gave him control over the territories of Arabia, Yemen, Najd and Bahrain, and Allāh said:

رِزْقُ رَبِّكَ خَيْرٌ وَّ اَبْقٰى

> **Whatever Allāh has given you, it is excellent and long lasting.** (*Ṭāhā*, 20:132)

The Holy Prophet[sa] also prophesied that Mecca and Medina would not go into the control of non-Muslims, who would be unaware of its sanctity. For 1,400 years this prophecy has held true. The country that Allāh had given to the Holy Prophet[sa] has always been under Muslim rule and non-Muslim powers have been unable to overcome it. There is no example of such a blessing in the world.

The spiritual blessing, or prophethood, has also been given to him in its best form as he has been given the title *Khātamun-Nabiyyīn* or *Seal of the Prophets*. This means that qualities reached their excellence in the Holy Prophet[sa], i.e. the qualities of prophethood that were found in other prophets individually were all combined and collectively appeared in the prophetethood of the Holy Prophet[sa]. In essence, there is no level or status of prophethood which was accomplished by any prophet that has not been given to the Holy Prophet[sa].

The title of Khātamun-Nabiyyīn is not only because of these collective qualities and because the Holy Prophet[sa] is better than all other prophets, but it is also because the grace of the Holy Prophet[sa] is better than all of the other prophets. Thus far, there is no other prophet through whom someone else could receive the blessings of prophethood. No other person has received prophethood while being a follower. This distinction has only been given to the Holy Prophet[sa] because he is Khātamun-Nabiyyīn. It is only through the Holy Prophet[sa] and by following him that a follower at the time of need can attain prophethood, and this matter is not against the verse of *Khātamun-Nabiyyīn*. Ḥaḍrat Imām Mullā 'Alī Qārī writes in his book *Mauḍū'āt-e-Kabīr*, that if Ibrāhīm[as], the son of the Holy Prophet[sa], lived or Ḥaḍrat 'Umar[ra] would have attained the blessings of prophethood, then they still would have been followers of the Holy Prophet[sa]. He says:

فلا يناقص قوله تعالیٰ وخاتم النبيين اذا المعنیٰ انه لا يأتی نبی بعده ينسخ ملته ولم يكن من امته

> This statement does not go against the title Seal of the Prophets, because the title means that there would be no prophet who would abrogate his Shariah, and a person cannot be a prophet who does not follow his law.
>
> (*Al-Mauḍū'ātil-Kubrā,* Mullā 'Alī Qārī, p. 192, Ḥadīth no. 745, Qadīmī Kutub Khānah Karachi)

Similarly, he says about the *ḥadīth,* 'There is no prophet after me,' that according to scholars, there would be no prophet who would abrogate the law that the Holy Prophet[sa] brought.

Imām Muḥammad Ṭāhir Sindhī has described the statement of Ḥaḍrat 'Ā'ishah[ra] that:

قولوا خاتم الانبياء ولا تقولوا لا نبی بعدہ

Call him Khātamul-Anbiyā' but do not say that there will not be any prophet after him.

(*Majma' Biḥārul-Anwār*, 'Allāmah Muḥammad Ṭāhir Gujrātī vol. 5, p. 502, under the word 'Zaid', Maktabah Dāril-Īmān, Madīnah Munawwarah, 1994)

Ḥaḍrat 'Ā'ishah[ra] has said this because there would be no prophet who would abrogate his *Shariah*.

The followers of a previous prophet could achieve three blessings by following him. They could become: *ṣiddīq* [*truthful*], *shahīd* [*martyr*], or *ṣāliḥ* [*righteous*]. But it was only due to the blessings of the Holy Prophet[sa] and by following him that a follower in the time of need could become a prophet. The Promised Messiah[as] writes:

یہ عجیب بات ہے کہ ہمارے سیدؐ و مولیٰ آنحضرت صلی اللہ علیہ وسلم کو جس قدر خدا تعالیٰ کی طرف سے نشان اور معجزات ملے۔ وہ صرف اُس زمانہ تک محدود نہ تھے بلکہ قیامت تک اُن کا سلسلہ جاری ہے۔ اور پہلے زمانوں میں جو کوئی نبی ہوتا تھا۔ وہ کسی گذشتہ نبی کی اُمّت نہیں کہلاتا تھا۔ گو اُس کے دین کی نصرت کرتا تھا اور اُس کو سچا جانتا تھا۔ مگر آنحضرت صلی اللہ علیہ وسلم کو یہ ایک خاص فخر دیا گیا ہے کہ وہ ان معنوں سے خاتم الانبیاء ہیں کہ ایک تو تمام کمالات نبوت اُن پر ختم ہیں۔ اور دوسرے یہ کہ اُن کے بعد کوئی نئی شریعت لانے والا رسول نہیں اور نہ کوئی ایسا نبی ہے جو اُن کی اُمّت سے باہر ہو۔ بلکہ ہر ایک کو جو شرف مکالمہ الٰہیہ ملتا ہے وہ انہیں کے فیض اور اُنہیں کی وساطت سے ملتا ہے اور وہ اُمتی کہلاتا ہے نہ کوئی مستقل نبی۔

It is a wonderful thing that our master the Holy Prophet (may peace and blessings of Allāh be upon him) was given miracles and signs that were not limited to his age but are continuous until the Day of Judgement. In previous times, when someone became a prophet, he was not considered from the ummah of the previous prophet, although he aided the prior prophet's religion and believed it to be true. On the other hand, the Holy Prophet (may peace and blessings of Allāh be upon him) was granted the special blessing that he became Khātamul-Anbiyā,' [Seal of the Prophets]; on one hand the qualities of prophethood were perfected in him and on the other hand there is no prophet who can bring a new law and come from outside his Ummah. Every person who achieves communication with God is only granted this through the blessings of the Holy Prophet[sa] and he is called a follower and not an independent prophet.

(*Statement attached to Chasma-e-Ma'rifat*, p. 8–9,
Rūḥānī Khazā'in, vol. 23, p. 380)

COUPLET 47

وَ اللّٰهِ إِنَّ مُحَمَّدًا كَرِدَافَةٍ
وَ بِهِ الْوُصُوْلُ بِسُدَّةِ السُّلْطَانِ

By God, Muḥammad[sa] is the vicegerent of God,
And through him alone can one reach the royal court of God.

This couplet is an explanation of the verse of the Holy Qur'ān:

ثُمَّ دَنَا فَتَدَلّٰى ۙ﴿۸﴾ فَكَانَ قَابَ قَوْسَيْنِ اَوْ اَدْنٰى ۚ﴿۹﴾

> **Then he drew nearer (to God), then he came down (to mankind), So that he became (as it were), one chord to two bows or closer still.** (*an-Najm,* 53:9-10)

This means that the Holy Prophet[sa] in his journey towards Allāh adopted the moral attributes of Allāh in such a perfect manner that he became very close to Allāh. Then he was sent down to the creatures of Allāh and dedicated all of his efforts towards the reformation and betterment of human beings.

The Promised Messiah says:

اس جگہ ایک ہی دل میں ایک ہی حالت اور نیت کے ساتھ دو قسم کا رجوع پایا گیا۔ ایک خدائے تعالیٰ کی طرف جو وجود قدیم ہے۔ اور ایک اس کے بندوں کی طرف جو وجود محدث ہے۔ اور دونوں قسم کا وجود یعنے قدیم اور حادث ایک دائرہ کی طرح ہے جس کی طرف اعلیٰ وجوب اور طرف اسفل امکان ہے۔ اب اس دائرہ کے درمیان میں انسان کامل بوجہ دنو اور تدلی کے دونوں طرف سے اتصال محکم کر کے یوں مثالی طور پر صورت پیدا کر لیتا ہے۔ جیسے ایک وتر دائرہ کے دو قوسوں میں ہوتا ہے یعنے حق اور خلق میں واسطہ ٹھہر جاتا ہے پہلے اس کو دنو اور قرب الٰہی کی خلعت خاص عطا کی جاتی ہے۔ اور قرب کے اعلیٰ مقام تک صعود کرتا ہے۔ اور پھر خلقت کی طرف اس کو لایا جاتا ہے۔ پس اس کا وہ صعود اور نزول دو قوس کی صورت میں ظاہر ہو جاتا ہے اور نفس جامع التعلقین انسان کامل کا ان دونوں قوسوں میں قاب قوسین کی طرح ہوتا ہے اور قاب

عرب کے محاورہ میں کمان کے چلے پر اطلاق پاتا ہے۔ پس آیت کے بطور تحت اللفظ یہ معنے ہوئے کہ نزدیک ہوا یعنے خدا سے۔ پھر اترا یعنے خلقت پر۔ پس اپنے اس صعود اور نزول کی وجہ سے دو قوسوں کے لئے ایک ہی وتر ہو گیا۔

Here, there were two diverse inclinations in one heart with the same mode and intention. One inclination was towards God who is Ever-Existing, and the other was towards His servants who are brought into existence through creation. Both kinds of entities - the Originator and the originated - are like a circle: its upper portion is the Higher Causation and the lower side is its contingent effect. In between the two, right in the middle is the perfect man who made a firm connection on both sides by ascending high to attain nearness to God, and then descending towards mankind. Thus, he took the likeness of one string that firmly joins two bows together; he was like a chord between two curves of a circle. He became a medium between God the Truth, and mankind. First, he received a distinctive station of closeness to God reaching the pinnacle of nearness to Him, and then he was brought down towards mankind. In this manner, his ascent and descent appeared in the shape of two curves; and thus the perfect man, in whose person both connections were flawlessly accomplished, is like *'qāba qausain'* – 'a chord between two bows.' In Arabic, the word *'qāb'* is applied to a bowstring. Therefore, the literal meaning of the verse (53:9) would be: 'He drew nearer, that is, to God, and then he came down to mankind, so that he became, as it were, one chord to two bows.'

(*Barāhīn-e-Aḥmadiyya,* part 4, *Rūḥānī Khazā'in*, vol. 1, p. 265, sub-footnote no. 1)

In this couplet the same subject has been related that the Holy Prophet[sa] is the intermediary between the Creator and the created. No one can achieve nearness to Allāh without following his religion. No action can be acceptable to Allāh without being followed through his religion and be in accordance with his *Shariah*, and performed in accordance with his *Sunnah*.

In the first couplet of this Qaṣīdah, it was explained that the only way to achieve nearness to Allāh was through the Holy Prophet[sa], and whoever does not drink from this spring is deprived forever because all other springs have dried up. In other words, with resorting to the Holy Prophet[sa] as a medium, no one can reach the Royal Court of Allah the Exalted.

COUPLET 48

هُوَ فَخْرُ كُلِّ مُطَهَّرٍ وَّ مُقَدَّسٍ
وَبِهٖ يُبَاهِى الْعَسْكَرُ الرُّوْحَانِيْ

He is the pride of the pious, the holiest;
He is the pride of the spiritual legions of men of virtue.

COUPLET 49

هُوَ خَيْرُ كُلِّ مُقَرَّبٍ مُّتَقَدِّمٍ
وَ الْفَضْلُ بِالْخَيْرَاتِ لَا بِزَمَانٖ

He excels all those who were close to God,
Indeed excellence is a matter of noble deeds, and not limited to time.

In the first part of the couplet, it is mentioned that the Holy Prophet[sa] is better and exalted than all the other people who achieved nearness to Allāh before him. The Promised Messiah says about his beloved, the Holy Prophet[sa]:

ہم جب انصاف کی نظر سے دیکھتے ہیں تو تمام سلسلہ نبوت میں سے اعلیٰ درجہ کا جوانمرد نبیؐ اور زندہ نبیؐ اور خدا کا اعلیٰ درجہ کا پیارا نبیؐ صرف ایک مرد کو جانتے ہیں یعنی وہی نبیوں کا سردار رسولوں کا فخر تمام مرسلوں کا سرتاج جس کا نام محمد مصطفٰے اور احمد مجتبٰی صلی اللہ علیہ وسلم ہے جس کے زیر سایہ دس دن چلنے سے وہ روشنی ملتی ہے جو پہلے اُس سے ہزار برس تک نہیں مل سکتی تھی۔

When we look into the matter with justice we find that throughout the system of prophethood there was only one prophet who was of an excellent calibre, brave, full of life, and the most dearest to God, who is the leader of all prophets, the pride of the prophets, the crown jewel of all the prophets, whose name is Muḥammad, the Chosen one, Aḥmad, the Elect [of God]. By

> following him, for only ten days, a person can attain such light, which could not have been achieved before in a thousand years.
> (*Sirāj-e-Munīr, Rūḥānī Khazā'in*, vol. 12, p. 82)

In the second part of the couplet another reason for his superiority is explained, in that there is no superiority in appearing earlier or later; rather, superiority depends upon the excellence of attributes and a high degree of actions that are fruitful. This same concept was expressed by Muḥammad Qāsim Nanautawī, founder of Dārul-'Ulūm, Deoband, when he was discussing Khātamun-Nabiyyīn in his book *Taḥdhīrun-Nās*:

> First of all we should understand the meanings of Khātamun-Nabiyyīn so we do not have a problem in understanding the concept. Among the general public it is understood that the Holy Prophet (may peace and blessings of Allāh be upon him) is *khātam* in the sense that his time was after the other prophets who came before him and therefore, he is the last prophet. But it is clear to the people of wisdom that there is no superiority merely because someone happened to be earlier or later in time. Also when Allāh says in his praise [29] وَ لٰكِنْ رَّسُوْلَ اللّٰهِ وَ خَاتَمَ النَّبِيّٖنَ it just cannot be correct. However, if you do not want to consider this as a meritorious compliment and that there is no intention of praise, then you can say he is khātam in the sense that he is last in time. But I know that from among the Muslims, no one will be able to

[29]...but he is the Messenger of Allah and the Seal of Prophets (*al-Aḥzāb*, 33:41)

accept my conclusion.

(*Taḥdhīrun-Nās,* Maulānā Muḥammad Qāsim Nānotwī, p. 41–42, Suhail Printers, Bilāl Ganj Lahore, Idāratul-'Azīz, Gujranwala, 3rd edition 2001)

Then he writes the essence of the words *Khātamun-Nabiyyīn* on page 57:

> From a physical fatherhood standpoint, the Holy Prophet (may peace and blessings of Allāh be upon him) has no superiority over any other man. However, in fatherhood of the righteous he is definitely superior and as far as the fatherhood of the prophets is concerned, the words Khātamun-Nabiyyīn are a witness over it.

Again he writes on pages 84–85:

> If you take the meaning of khātam as I am presenting – signifying personal attributes and attributes of prophethood, then we can say that there is no person who has achieved the level of the Holy Prophet (may peace and blessings of Allāh be upon him). Actually in this viewpoint, not only does he become superior to the prophets before him, he becomes superior to the people after him. Even if a prophet is raised after the Holy Prophet (may peace and blessings of Allāh be upon him) it will not make any difference to his being khātam.

In this couplet the superiority of the Holy Prophet (may peace and blessings of Allāh be upon him) is mentioned because he is a composite of the attributes of all people who were close to Allāh, and timing has nothing to do with his superiority, but is dependent upon the excellence of attributes and achievements. Therefore, irrespective of the era in which the Holy Prophet[sa] existed, and irrespective of the number of people who would attain divine nearness after him, the Holy Prophet[sa] would remain supreme.

COUPLET 50

وَ الطَّلُّ قَدْ يَبْدُوْ أَمَامَ الْوَابِلِ
فَا لطَّلُّ طَلٌّ لَّيْسَ كَا لتَّهْتَانِ

Reflect! The drizzle precedes the heavy rain.
Yet drizzle is drizzle and rain is rain.

In this couplet, a question is being answered that if the Holy Prophet[sa] is superior to all the previous prophets, then what is the status of the prophets who were sent to the people by Allāh in the past. The writer of the Qaṣīdah explains that they were similar to a light rain that signifies that a heavier rain is about to come. In the same manner, the previous prophets came to give the glad tidings that the Holy Prophet[sa] was going to appear. They were all entrusted to foretell only that the leader of the prophets, their jewel, the Seal of the Prophets, king of humanity, Ḥaḍrat Muḥammad[sa] was about to appear.

COUPLET 51

بَطَلٌ وَّحِيْدٌ لَّا تَطِيْشُ سِهَامُهُ
ذُوْ مُصْمِيَاتٍ مُوْبِقُ الشَّيْطَانِ

He is the unchallenged archer. His arrows do not miss the target,
They are dead set on killing Satan.

Allāh had blessed the Holy Prophet[sa] with such awe and fear that the enemy did not have the strength to face him. One time Abū Jahl, who was renowned for bravery amongst the Meccans, owed money to a person and would not pay him back. Some Meccans said to that person that he should go and see Muḥammad[sa] about this matter. It was a mischievous plan, that on one hand if the Holy Prophet[sa] did not help he would be guilty of breaking his oath which is known as *Ḥilful-Fuḍūl*, and on the other hand, if he went with this man to Abū Jahl, then he was sure to be harmed. When this lender came to the Holy Prophet[sa] and asked for his help, the Holy Prophet[sa] went with him without any hesitation and knocked the door of Abū Jahl. Abū Jahl responded and came out. The Holy Prophet[sa] asked him to pay his debt. Without any delay or hesitation, Abū Jahl paid his debt on the spot. The leaders of Mecca later taunted Abū Jahl by reminding him that he was the one who used to tell them to harass the Holy Prophet[sa], and now he had humbly obeyed him. Abū Jahl answered them that I swear by God that if you were in my place you would have done the same thing. I saw two mad camels on both sides of Muḥammad[sa] ready to attack a and kill me by twisting my neck.

(*As-Sīratun-Nabawiyyah,* Ibni Hishām, Amrul-Arāshī Alladhī Bā'a Abā Jahlin Ibilahū, p. 420–421, Dārul-Kutubil-'Ilmiyyah, Beirut, 2001)

The awe of truth that radiated from the Holy Prophet[sa] trampled mischief, and all others had to succumb to this power of truth.

COUPLET 52

هُوَ جَنَّةٌ إِنِّیْ أَرٰی أَثْمَارَهٗ
وَقُطُوْفَهٗ قَدْ ذُلِّلَتْ لِجَنَانِیْ

He is a garden and I see that his fruits
and clusters have been brought within the easy reach of my heart.

In this couplet the Promised Messiah[as] says that his own heart has a very powerful relationship with the heart of the Holy Prophet[sa]. That is the reason he has received blessings from him. This relationship has been mentioned in one of Promised Messiah's revelations:

کُل برکة من محمد صلی اللّٰہ علیہ وسلم فتبارک من علّم وتعلّم۔

The source of every blessing is Muḥammad[sa]; a blessed one has taught and a blessed one has learned.

(*Barāhīn-e-Aḥmadiyya,* part 1, *Rūḥānī Khazā'in,* vol. 1, p. 265, Sub-footnote no. 1)

In other words, the Holy Prophet[sa] is his teacher and guide, and the Promised Messiah[as] is his pupil.

COUPLET 53

أَلْفَيْتُهُ بَحْرَ الْحَقَائِقِ وَالْهُدٰى
وَرَأَيْتُهُ كَالدُّرِّ فِي اللَّمَعَانِ

I found him to be an ocean of truth and guidance;
I found him to be a pearl of lustre and light.

Allāh taught the Holy Prophet[sa] knowledge and facts which were not apparent to the rest of the world. For example, the Holy Prophet[sa] said that there is a cure for every disease except death. He made this statement at a time when many diseases were considered incurable. After years and years of research, we find that many 'incurable' diseases have now become curable. In the same manner he stated once by a revelation of Allāh,

خلق لكم ما في الارض جميعا۔ [30]

and another revelation:

[30] *He it is Who has created for you all that is in the earth. al-Baqarah*, 2:30, (Publishers)

رَبَّنَا مَا خَلَقْتَ هٰذَا بَاطِلًا۔[31]

Everything in this world has been created for the benefit of human beings. We find that in this age many things have been found to be beneficial that were considered previously harmful or useless.

The Promised Messiah[as] says about the Holy Prophet[sa].

بر لبش جاری ز حکمت چشمۂ
در دلش پُر از معارف کوثرے
امی و در علم و حکمت بے نظیر
زیں چہ باشد حجتی روشن ترے

This means that from his mouth there is a fountain of wisdom that continuously flows. His heart is a pure river of knowledge. He is unlettered but his wisdom is unparalleled. What other proof is needed for his truthfulness?

(*Barāhīn-e-Aḥmadiyya*, part 1, *Rūḥānī Khazā'in*, vol. 1, p. 18–19)

---

[31] O Our Lord, you have not created this in vain. *Āl-e-'Imrān*, 3:192, (Publishers)

COUPLET 54

قَدْ مَاتَ عِيْسٰى مُطْرِقًا وَ نَبِيُّنَا
حَيٌّ وَ رَبِّیْ إِنَّــهٗ وَافَانِیْ

Jesus silently bowed his head, and died. As for our Prophet,
He is alive, and by my Lord, he has met me.

In the previous couplets the past prophets were likened to the light rain that preceded and foretold of a heavier rain (*Sūrah al-Baqarah* أَوْ كَصَيِّبٍ مِّنَ السَّمَآءِ ـ[32] represents Islam and the advent of the Holy Prophet[sa] as a heavy rain.), and that the composite of all the attributes of the earlier prophets was found in the personality of the Holy Prophet[sa].

Now a question arises that the Christians believe the same thing about Jesus. They consider him to be superior to all the prophets, and *the Seal of the Prophets.* The writer priest named Būtāmal of the booklet *Khātamun-Nabiyyīn*, published by Punjab Religious Book Society, 2nd edition in 1953 says:

> It is only the Israelites that were selected to receive and deliver the word of God, therefore the advent of the Seal of the Prophets was to take place from the Children of Israel, and that last prophet is Jesus Christ. It is this very last prophet who put a seal on

[32] *al-Baqarah*, 2:20

> prophethood and revelation by saying that it is finished. (*Khātamun-Nabiyyīn*, p. 5)

Then on page 10 he writes:

> This world has been left as an open ground for false prophets until the second advent of our God Jesus so people can be tried.

Again on page 21 he writes:

> Therefore, our research forces us to declare to the world that according to the Torah, the Prophets, and the Gospel, after our God Jesus and his disciples, there is no prophecy of any other prophet to appear in the future. Therefore, after Jesus and his disciples, anyone's claim of prophethood is not to be credible and accepted.

The Christians say that Jesus was raised to the heavens alive where he has been living for the past 2,000 years. They also believe that Jesus will appear in the latter days and will guide the world to the right path. Muslims have similar beliefs that he will kill the antichrist, destroy Gog and Magog, and will achieve the level of success that no other prophet has achieved. In considering all of the above, it is not proper to give superiority to anyone over Jesus. This couplet answers this very question, where the Promised Messiah[as] says that Jesus is dead, but our Holy Prophet[sa] is still living.

I consider it proper to mention a dialogue that took place between me and a Syrian person who was the attorney of the missionary In-Charge of Syria, Mr. Alfred Nelson Dimurkey. It was the beginning of 1926 in Damascus and he came to see me at my home, and wanted to discuss religious topics. I inquired as to what topic he wanted to discuss. He responded, the subject of the superiority of Muḥammad[sa] or Jesus[as]. I asked him if he wanted to discuss it according to the Qur'ān or the Gospels and his response was according to the Qur'ān.

I told him that according to the Holy Qur'ān, the status of Christ to Muḥammad[sa] is as a pupil to his teacher. He was very astonished at my comment so I invited him to mention a verse which gives him the impression that Jesus was superior. He said the Qur'ān says the angel of God gave glad tidings to Mary: لِاَهَبَ لَكِ غُلٰمًا زَكِيًّا meaning, you would be given a pure boy. No other prophet has been mentioned in the Holy Qur'ān as being pure, meaning sinless and without any blemish. He further stated that the fact that the word *zakī* [*pure*] is used only for Jesus and not for any other prophet implies that Jesus was the only one pure and innocent, and no other prophet shares this attribute with him.

I answered him that if the same word were to be used in the Holy Qur'ān about the Holy Prophet[sa] then it would have been proven that the Holy Prophet[sa] and Jesus[as] are of equal status. However, I have stated to you that the Holy Prophet[sa] is as a teacher and Jesus as his pupil. In the Holy Qur'ān the word *muzakkī* is used from the same root as you have mentioned and supports my claim, Allāh says in *Sūrah al-Jumu'ah*:

هُوَ الَّذِیْ بَعَثَ فِی الْاُمِّیّٖنَ رَسُوْلًا مِّنْهُمْ یَتْلُوْا عَلَیْهِمْ اٰیٰتِهٖ وَ یُزَكِّیْهِمْ [33]

[33] *al-Jumu'ah,* 62:3

This means that the Holy Prophet[sa] has been sent to an unlettered people and he teaches them signs and purifies them. In this verse the Holy Prophet[sa] has been mentioned as one who makes others *zakī*, i.e., one who transforms others into the likeness of Jesus Christ. I told him that he was under the wrong impression that according to the Holy Qur'ān Jesus[as] is superior to all prophets including the Holy Prophet[sa]; and it should be clear to him that according to this verse the status of the Holy Prophet[sa] is that of a teacher and of Jesus[as] as a pupil. Jesus[as] is referred to as a *zakī* and the Holy Prophet[sa] as a *muzakkī*, meaning the one who makes others *zakī*.

Upon my questioning him further, he presented another verse in which he said the Holy Qur'ān has mentioned about the purity of the ancestors of Jesus Christ. His point was that there is no mention of the ancestry of Muḥammad[sa] at all. I asked him: 'Do you consider the Qur'ān to be the word of God or of Muḥammad[sa]?'

He answered: 'Of Muḥammad[sa].'

So I responded: 'Then who do you think purified the name of the ancestors of Jesus? Even by this logic the Holy Prophet[sa] is established as a *muzakkī* which is the status of the teacher.'

Then I explained to him that his understanding of this verse is incorrect. The Holy Qur'ān is not a book of family trees where the forefathers of all prophets had to be mentioned. The mention of the forefathers of Jesus[as] was for the reason that his ancestors were blemished. Even in the Gospels, in the book of Matthew, chapter 1, verses 3 and 6, where the family tree of Jesus has been mentioned, two of his grandmothers have been mentioned as committing adultery. When Allāh mentioned Jesus[as] to be a prophet in the Holy Qur'ān He added that his forefathers were also pure and clean. It is obvious that a cloth which is white and spotless does not need any cleaning. On the other hand, if it is dirty and has stains on it, it has to be washed and cleaned. The ancestors of the Holy Prophet[sa] were known among the people to be pure and clean, and therefore, there was no need to comment further upon them. If I take your line of thinking then from the verse وَمَا كَفَرَ سُلَيْمٰنُ (Solomon was not a disbeliever) we can conclude, that God forbid, Jesus[as] was a disbeliever because in the verse it says that Ḥaḍrat Solomon[as] was not one of the disbelievers, but it does not mention the same thing about Jesus. The fact of the matter is that Ḥaḍrat Solomon[as] had to be cleared of this blame of being a disbeliever and being guilty of *shirk*.

(*See 1st book of Kings*, ch.11, v.1-11)

The third verse he presented was in which the Holy Qur'ān says about Jesus[as] اَيَّدْنٰهُ بِرُوْحِ الْقُدُسِ meaning, that Allāh assisted him with the Holy Spirit. I told him that the Holy Qur'ān says about Adam:

وَ نَفَخْتُ فِيْهِ مِنْ رُّوْحِىْ فَقَعُوْا لَهٗ سٰجِدِيْنَ

Meaning, I have breathed into him of My Spirit, fall thee down in submission to him, so the angels submitted to him. (al-Ḥijr 15:30).

We find in no place where the angels submitted to Jesus[as]. We do find in the Gospel of Mathew where it is written that one time Satan asked Jesus[as] to submit to him.

The meaning of the Holy Spirit is the Angel Gabriel. In a *Ḥadīth* we find that the Holy Prophet[sa] said to Ḥassān bin Thābit[ra], اَنْشِدْ وروح القدس معک 'Recite your poetry and may the Holy Spirit be with you.'

In the Holy Qur'ān we find that Allāh says about the companions of the Holy Prophet[sa] وَ اَيَّدَهُمْ بِرُوْحٍ مِّنْهُ that Allāh assisted them with the Holy Spirit. Now the companions of the Holy Prophet[sa] were his pupils and as Jesus[as] was also assisted by the Holy Spirit, again this shows him to be a pupil as compared to the Holy Prophet[sa].

Allāh says about the Holy Prophet[sa] [34] عَلَّمَهٗ شَدِيْدُ الْقُوٰى that he was taught by *Shadīdul-Quwā*, which is a manifestation of Gabriel. The Holy Spirit is also a manifestation of Gabriel. According to the Gospels, the Holy Spirit descended upon Jesus[as] in the shape of a dove.[35] We find in a *Ḥadīth* that when Gabriel appeared to the Holy Prophet[sa], the whole sky was filled with his manifestation.[36] There is no comparison between these great manifestations as compared to that of a dove.

Then he said that you believe that Jesus has been raised to the skies according to [37] بَلْ رَّفَعَهُ اللّٰهُ اِلَيْهِ and he is still living and will descend in the latter days; however, Muḥammad[sa] died as other human beings do. I said that you are not aware of my belief. I believe that Jesus[as] has died and the Holy Prophet Muḥammad[sa] is alive. He astonishingly asked me: *'How is that?'*

---

[34] *An-Najm*, 53:6

[35] Matthew 3:16

[36] Ṣaḥīḥul-Bukhārī, Kitābul-Bad'il-Waḥyi, ch.3, Ḥadīth no.4

[37] *An-Nisā'*, 4:159

I said that from a physical sense, all prophets have died, and the word *rafa'a* in the mentioned verse refers to an elevated status and nearness to Allāh. Since the Jews claimed that they had killed Jesus on the cross and therefore established him as being accursed of God, Allāh states that the Jews killed him neither on the cross nor in any other manner. Therefore, he is not accursed but has a close relationship with Allāh. In the Arabic language, if the word *rafa'a* is used when the subject is Allāh and the object is a human being, there is no other meaning of this word except nearness to Allāh and elevation in status. Forget about the heavens, it cannot mean elevating anyone even upon a hill.

In the Holy Qur'ān in Sūrah A'rāf, it says:

وَلَوْ شِئْنَا لَرَفَعْنٰهُ بِهَا وَلٰكِنَّهٗٓ اَخْلَدَ اِلَى الْاَرْضِ وَاتَّبَعَ هَوٰىهُ

And if we had so desired, we could have exalted him thereby, but he inclined to the earth, and followed his evil inclination (*al-A'rāf,* 7:177)

In this verse even the word 'earth' has been mentioned with *rafa'a,* but no one attempts to imply the meaning of 'taking him up to the skies.'

In a *ḥadīth* it says:

إذا تواضع العبدُ رفعهُ اللهُ إلى السّماء السّابعة

Meaning, when a person shows humility, Allāh elevates him to the seventh heaven.

(*Kanzul-'Ummāl Fī Sunanil-Aqwāli Wal-Af'āl,* Kitābul-Akhlāqi Qismul-Aqwāl, vol. 3, p. 49, Ḥadīth no. 5717, Dārul-Kutubil-'Ilmiyyah, Beirut, 2001)

In spite of the fact that the word 'heaven' is used along with *rafa'a*, no one takes the literal meaning that a person showing humility is taken up literally to the heavens. As I have mentioned before in the Arabic language *rafa' ilallāh* only means nearness to Allāh and elevation of status and not bodily elevation so you should not get the wrong impression from the word *rafa'*.

I further stated that the Holy Prophet[sa] has also died in a physical sense, but from the perspective of spiritual benefits and blessings, he is alive and Jesus[as] is dead. No one can achieve nearness to Allāh to the point of having communication with Him by following Jesus[as]. Neither his religion nor religious law is alive today and has no spiritual benefits. On the other hand, the spiritual benefits of the Holy Prophet[sa] and his powers of purification are continuing. People are benefiting from it today. His religion is alive, his book is alive, and his law is alive. Therefore, it is only the Holy Prophet[sa] who can be considered and declared as being the only living prophet.

Upon hearing all of this he said this is all new to him. Then he discussed a little while longer and left.

COUPLETS 55, 56 AND 57

وَ اللهِ إِنِّیْ قَدْ رَأَیْتُ جَمَالَهٗ
بِعُیُوْنِ جِسْمِیْ قَاعِدًا بِمَکَانِیْ

I call Allāh to witness that I have seen his beauty,
With my physical eyes in my own home.

هَا إِنْ تَظَنَّیْتَ ابْنَ مَرْیَمَ عَائِشًا
فَعَلَیْكَ إِثْبَاتًا مِّنَ الْبُرْهَانِ

Look! If you think that Jesus is alive,
Then produce your proof, if you have any!

أَفَأَنْتَ لَاقَیْتَ الْمَسِیْحَ بِیَقْظَةٍ
أَوْ جَاءَكَ الْأَنْبَآءُ مِنْ یَّقْظَانِ

Have you ever seen Jesus while you were awake?
Or has any living man claimed to have seen him?

COUPLET 58

أُنْظُرْ إِلَى الْقُرْآنِ كَيْفَ يُبَيِّنُ
أَفَأَنْتَ تُعْرِضُ عَنْ هُدَى الرَّحْمٰنِ

Look at the Qur'ān how clearly it declares his death.
Would you turn away from the guidance of the Gracious God?

The above two couplets are addressed mainly to the Muslims who believe that Jesus is alive in the heavens and that he will come down in some unknown period of time. This belief is a great advantage for Christians to lead people astray.

The writer of this Qaṣīdah says in his Persian poetry:

مسیح ناصری را تا قیامت زندہ می فہمند
مگر مدفون یثرب را ندادند ایں فضیلت را
زبوئے نافۂ عرفاں چو محروم ازل بووند
پسندیدند در شانِ شہِ خلق ایں مذلت را
ہمہ دُر ہائے قرآں را چو خاشا کے .بیفگندند
ز علم ناتمام شاں چہاگم گشت ملت را
ہمہ عیسائیاں را از مقالِ خودمدد دادند
دلیری ہا پدید آمد پرستارانِ میّت را

This means that people consider Jesus to be living until the Day of Judgment but they do not assign this superior position to Ḥaḍrat Muḥammad[sa] who is buried in Yathrib. Since these people lack the fragrance of spiritual wisdom and knowledge, they accepted this inferiority for the Holy Prophet[sa]. They cast all of the pearls of the Holy Qur'ān in the dirt. The Islamic nation experienced great losses because of their inferior knowledge. Because of their above-mentioned belief, they aided the Christians, and a man-worshipping nation became aggressive in their propagation.[38]

DEATH OF JESUS[AS]:

The death of Jesus[as] is apparent from many verses of the Holy Qur'ān. A few of them are listed here as examples. First verse:

وَ اِذْ قَالَ اللّٰهُ يٰعِيْسَى ابْنَ مَرْيَمَ ءَاَنْتَ قُلْتَ لِلنَّاسِ اتَّخِذُوْنِيْ
وَ اُمِّيَ اِلٰهَيْنِ مِنْ دُوْنِ اللّٰهِ ۔

And when Allāh will say: "O Jesus, son of Mary, didst thou say to men, 'Take me and my mother for two gods besides Allāh... (*al-Mā'idah*, 5:117)
He will reply:

مَا قُلْتُ لَهُمْ اِلَّا مَآ اَمَرْتَنِيْ بِهٖٓ اَنِ اعْبُدُوا اللّٰهَ رَبِّيْ وَ رَبَّكُمْ ۚ وَ كُنْتُ عَلَيْهِمْ شَهِيْدًا
مَّا دُمْتُ فِيْهِمْ ۚ فَلَمَّا تَوَفَّيْتَنِيْ كُنْتَ اَنْتَ الرَّقِيْبَ عَلَيْهِمْ ۔

[38] *Ā'īna'-e-Kamālāt-e-Islām*, *Rūḥānī Khazā'in*, vol. 5, p. 56

> **I said nothing to them except that which Thou didst command me 'Worship Allāh, my Lord and your Lord.' And I was a witness over them as long as I remained among them, but since Thou didst cause me to die, Thou hast been the Watcher over them; and Thou art Witness over all things.** (*al-Mā'idah*, 5:118)

To paraphrase, this means that I do not know when they made me and my mother the subject of their worship and how it came about, in any case it did not happen in my lifetime when I was a witness and present among them.

In this verse, the death of Jesus is proven in a very clear manner. It is described in this verse that Jesus[as] would mention to Allāh two different periods of time. One, when he was present in his nation and the second, when he was absent. In the middle of these two periods, the word *tawaffaitanī* (when you caused me to die) reflects that it was his death that separated these two periods. So it is very clear that his absence from his nation was a result of his death. And this proves very clearly that he has died.

This argument is validated by a *ḥadīth* reported in Ṣaḥīḥ Bukhārī. In fact, Ḥaḍrat Imām Bukhārī himself used this *ḥadīth* in his commentary to explain the above mentioned verse. The *ḥadīth* says that the Holy Prophet[sa] said that on the Day of Judgment, some of my companions would be caught and taken away and I would say these are my companions!

فيقال انک لاتدری ما احدثوا بعدک فاقول کما قال العبد الصالح وَكُنْتُ عَلَيْهِمْ شَهِيْدًا مَّا دُمْتُ فِيْهِمْ فَلَمَّا تَوَفَّيْتَنِىْ كُنْتَ أَنْتَ الرَّقِيْبَ عليهم فيقال ان هؤلاء لم يزالو مرتدين على اعقابهم منذ فارقتهم

Then he would be answered that you do not know what they did after you had gone. You do not know what type of innovations they came up with. The Holy Prophet[sa] says that I will say the same thing that the righteous servant of Allāh has been reported to have said in the Holy Qur'ān that I was a guardian and witness over them as long as I was among them but when you caused me to die, you alone were the watcher over them. Then it would be said to the Holy Prophet[sa], that as soon as you departed from them, they turned away from their religion.

(*Ṣaḥīḥul-Bukhāri,* Kitābut-Tafsīr, under Sūrah al-Mā'idah, Bāb Wa Kuntu 'Alaihim Shahīdan, Ḥadīth no.4625)

From this *ḥadīth* the meaning of the words of Jesus[as] *fallamā tawaffaitanī* becomes clear. It becomes apparent that just as these companions of the Holy Prophet[sa] turned away from Islam after the death of the Holy Prophet[sa], in the same manner the practice of worshipping Jesus[as] spread among the Christians after the death of Jesus. Therefore, from this verse it becomes very clear and certain that Jesus is not living and has died.

SECOND VERSE:

وَمَا مُحَمَّدٌ إِلَّا رَسُولٌ ۚ قَدْ خَلَتْ مِن قَبْلِهِ الرُّسُلُ ۗ أَفَإِن مَّاتَ أَوْ قُتِلَ انقَلَبْتُمْ عَلَىٰ أَعْقَابِكُمْ ۚ

And Muḥammad is only a messenger. Verily, (all) messengers have passed away before him. If then he die or be slain, will you turn back on your heels? *(Āl-e-'Imrān, 3:145)*

In this verse, Allāh has given the news to the Holy Prophet[sa] that all of the prophets before him, which includes Jesus[as], have died. Furthermore, the only two means of passing away of the prophets are described as death or murder. If there were a third means such as ascending to heaven, then it should have been included in this verse. So this verse also proves the death of Jesus because he is one of the prophets who appeared before the Holy Prophet[sa] in time.

CONSENSUS OF THE COMPANIONS:

Ṣaḥīḥ Bukhārī[39] mentions that when the Holy Prophet[sa] died and the news of his passing away started to spread in Medina, the companions were in denial and shock. Ḥaḍrat 'Umar[ra] threatened to kill anyone who said that the Holy Prophet[sa] had died. On that day Ḥaḍrat Abū Bakr[ra] delivered a sermon in which he stated:

---

[39] *Ṣaḥīḥul-Muslim,* Kitābul-Maghāzī, Bābu Maraḍin-Nabiyyi Wa Wafātihī, Ḥadīth no. 4454

مَن كَانَ مِنكُم يَعبُدُ مُحَمّداً فَإِنَّ مُحَمَّداً قد مَاتَ وَمَن كَانَ مِنكُم يَعبُدُ الله فان الله حيٌّ لا يَمُوتُ۔ قَالَ اللهُ وَمَا مُحَمَّدٌ إِلَّا رَسُولٌ قَدْ خَلَتْ مِن قَبْلِهِ الرُّسُل أَفَإِن مَّاتَ أَوْ قُتِلَ انقَلَبْتُمْ عَلَىٰ أَعْقَابِكُم۔

> Anyone among you who worshipped Muḥammad should hear this – Muḥammad has died – and whoever among you worships Allāh should know that Allāh will live forever and shall never experience death. Allāh has stated that Muḥammad is only a messenger of Allāh and all of the prophets before him have died (he recited the whole verse mentioned above.)

There is another *ḥadīth* which states:

فتلقّاها منه الناس كلهم فما اسمع بشراً من الناس الا يتلوها

> Meaning, All the people memorized this verse after they listened to Abū Bakr and the narrator says that he could hear almost everyone reciting this verse on that day.
>
> (*Ṣaḥīḥul-Muslim,* Kitābul-Maghāzī, Bābu Maraḍin-Nabiyyi Wa Wafātihī, Ḥadīth no. 4454)

Ḥaḍrat ʻUmar[ra] states that as soon as Abū Bakr[ra] recited this verse, I was in such a state of shock and sorrow that I could not stand up and fell down to my knees and finally accepted that the Holy Prophet[sa] had passed away.

At that time if Ḥaḍrat ʻUmar[ra] or any other companion believed that Jesus[as] was alive bodily in heaven, what would have prevented their questioning why Jesus[as], who was also a prophet, was still alive? But none of the companions raised this question. The fact that none of the companions, and especially Ḥaḍrat 'Umar[ra], did not mention the example of Jesus[as] and accepted the argument relating to the death of the Holy Prophet[sa] which was proven by the verse that all prophets before the Holy Prophet[sa] had died, is a clear proof of their belief that all prophets before the Holy Prophet[sa], including Jesus[as], had died.

HISTORY:

When we examine the history of Islam it becomes clear that even if a person was perplexed about Jesus' death owing to Christian influence before the death of the Holy Prophet[sa], there was no doubt left on this issue at the time of the death of the Holy Prophet[sa]. All the companions of the Holy Prophet[sa] accepted with full certainty that all prophets had passed away from this world.

The apostates used the death of the Holy Prophet[sa] as a reason to reject him. They started to say:

لو كان محمدٌ نبيًّا لما مات۔

If Muḥammad was a prophet then he should not have died.
(*Tārīkhur-Rusuli Wal-Mulūk, Tārikhuṭ-Ṭabarī,* Abū Ja'far Muḥammad bin Jarīr Aṭ-Ṭabarī, vol. 4, p. 3, Dhikru Khabari Ahlil-Baḥrain Wa Raddatil-Ḥuṭami, Dārul-Fikr, Beirut, edition 2002)

The answer to this question was already given in the Holy Qur'ān that since all prophets before him passed away, the death of the

Holy Prophet^{sa} does not negate his prophethood. However, this propaganda of the enemies spread throughout many tribes. The tribes of Bahrain and Ḥaṭam became apostates only on the issue that Muḥammad^{sa} being a prophet had died. The famous historian Ibni Jarīr Aṭ-Ṭabarī writes about the tribe of Jārūd bin Mu'allā named 'Abdul-Qais:

> They had accepted Islam a very short time before the Holy Prophet^{sa} passed away. His tribesmen said that if Muḥammad^{sa} was a prophet he should not have died and they turned away from Islam. When Jārūd learned about this, he gathered all the people together and said to them, 'O people of 'Abdul-Qais, I am about to ask you something and I would like you to provide me the answer.' They said: 'Ask whatever you desire. Jārūd asked them if they knew whether Allah sent prophets to the world in previous times.' They answered: 'Yes.' Then Jārūd asked them what happened to them. They answered that they all died. Then Jārūd said: 'Just as the previous prophets left this world, Muḥammad^{sa} has died.' He declared that day that:
>
> لا اِلهَ اِلَّا اللهُ وَاَنَّ مُحَمَّدًا عَبْدُهُ وَرَسُولُهُ
>
> 'There is none worthy of worship except Allāh and Muḥammad^{sa} is His servant and messenger.' His tribesmen said that we also bear witness that there is no god but Allāh and certainly Muḥammad^{sa} is His messenger and His servant, and we consider you our elder and our leader.

The whole tribe then became firm in Islam.
(*Tārīkh-e-Ṭabarī*, vol. 1, part.4, p. 94–95, Urdu translation, printed in Hyderabad, Dakkan)

From this historical event it becomes clear that the apostates at the time of the Holy Prophet[sa] used his death as the basis of their apostasy. Their argument was rejected based upon the fact that all prophets before the Holy Prophet[sa] had died. It is apparent that this argument could only work if every one of the prophets before him had passed away, because even if one person was considered to be alive, then the argument fails. Thus it was the consensus of the companions of the Holy Prophet[sa] that Jesus had in fact died.

Later, when Islam spread amongst the Christian nations, and the Christians accepted Islam in large numbers, their proper religious training could not take place. Due to the Christian influence, Muslims started to spread the same beliefs that were in existence before Islam. Also, since the Christians and Jews were considered to be educated and learned people, the Muslim public started to listen to them after they accepted Islam and slowly began to interpret the verses of the Holy Qurʾān in line with their thinking. For example, in the commentary of Wahab bin Mambah, under the commentary of the verse: *innī mutawaffīka wa rāfiʿuka ilayya* (إِنِّي مُتَوَفِّيكَ وَرَافِعُكَ إِلَيَّ) it states that Allāh gave Jesus death for three days and then He revived him and then raised him to heaven:

اماتهُ اللهُ ثلاثةَ ايامٍ ثمّ رفعهُ.[40]

---

[40] *Tafsīrul-Qurʾānil-ʿAẓīm*, Ibni Kathīr, vol. 2, p. 39, Tafsīru Sūrah Āl-e-ʿImrān, under verse no. 56, Dārul-Kutubil-ʿIlmiyyah, Beirut, 2004

In the same way, Sa'īd bin Al-Muṣayyib, writes in his commentary of the same verse:

رُفعَ عیسٰی وھو ابن ثلاث وثلاثین سنۃ۔ رفعہُ اللّٰہُ من بیت المقدس۔

> Jesus was raised up at the age of 33 and his ascension took place at Baitul-Maqdas, Jerusalem.
>
> (*Fatḥul-Bayān,* vol. 2, p. 247, Tafsīr Sūrah Āl-e-'Imrān, under verse 56, Al-Maktabul-'Aṣariyyah, Beirut 1992)

Whatever has been stated in these two commentaries is exactly from the Gospels. (Mark chapter 45; Luke chapter 24; and Acts chapter 1, verse 2)

The writer of the commentary *Fatḥul-Bayān* states that the ascension of Jesus[as] at the age of 33 is not verified by any saying of the Holy Prophet[sa]. He writes that Imām Shāmī has stated:

و ھو کما قال فانّ ذلک انما یروی عن النصاریٰ والمصرح
بہ فی الاحادیث النبویّۃ انّہٗ انما رفع وھو ابن مائۃ وعشرین سنۃ۔

> Imām Ibni Qayyim is correct because this belief is of the Christians and in the ḥadīth of the Holy Prophet[sa] it is clearly mentioned that Jesus was raised up in the age of 120.
>
> (*Fatḥul-Bayān,* vol. 2, p. 247, Tafsīr Sūrah Āl-e-'Imrān, under verse 56, Al-Maktabul-'Aṣariyyah, Beirut 1992)

Our stance is that the *ḥadīth* states that Jesus lived to be 120 years old at the same time the Holy Prophet[sa] stated that his age would be half that of Jesus.[41] However, there is no mention of ascension in this *ḥadīth*. The belief about the ascension of Jesus[as] was introduced to the Muslims from newly converted Christians as we have explained above. It was certainly not the belief of the Holy Prophet[sa] or his companions. They were all believers in the death of Jesus. As a matter of fact, the first imam among the four imams of *fiqh* [religious jurisprudence], Ḥaḍrat Imām Mālik, who passed away in year 179 after *hijrah*, was a believer in the death of Jesus[as].

Imām Muḥammad Ṭāhir Gujrātī, writes in Majma'ul-Bihār, volume 1, page 286:

والاکثر انؑ عیسٰی لم یمت وقال مالک مات۔

> Generally people say that Jesus has not died but Imām Mālik's belief was that Jesus had died.
>
> (*Majma' Biḥārul-Anwār,* 'Allāmah Muḥammad Ṭāhir Gujrātī, vol. 1, p. 534, under the word 'Ḥakam', Maktabah Dāril-Īmān, Madīnah Munawwarah, 1994)

Sheikh Sa'dī has stated correctly in his Persian couplet:

بدنیا گر کسے پائندہ بودے

ابو القاسم محمدؐ زندہ بودے

If anyone were worthy of everlasting life,

[41] *Kanzul-'Ummāl Fī Sunanil-Aqwāli Wal-Af'āl,* Kitābul-Faḍā'ili, Faḍā'ilu Sā'iril-Anbiyā'i Ṣalawātullāhi....., vol. 11, p. 217, Ḥadīth no. 32,259, Dārul-Kutubil-'Ilmiyyah, Beirut, 2001

It would be Abul-Qāsim Muḥammad[sa].

COUPLET 59

فَاعْلَمْ بِاَنَّ الْعَيْشَ لَيْسَ بِثَابِتٍ
بَلْ مَاتَ عِيْسٰى مِثْلَ عَبْدٍ فَانٍ

Know that there is no proof of his life.
Indeed Jesus died as all mortal men die.

In the *Dīwān-e-Khansā'*, it states that one time Ḥaḍrat Khansā' was crying over the passing away of her brother and Ḥaḍrat 'Umar[ra] passed by her house. Ḥaḍrat 'Umar[ra] consoled her and told her to be patient and said:

لو خلد احدٌ لخلد رسول الله صلى الله عليه وسلم

If any person would have been allowed to live forever, it would have been the Holy Prophet[sa].
(*Majallatu Lughatil-'Arabil-'Irāqiyyah,* Editor Kāẓim Ad-Dujailī, part.9, p. 563–564, 'Khansā', Quoted by Maktabah Shāmilah CD)

In the same way, Allāh says in the Holy Qur'ān:

وَمَا جَعَلْنَا لِبَشَرٍ مِّنْ قَبْلِكَ الْخُلْدَ ؕ اَفَاۡئِنْ مِّتَّ فَهُمُ الْخٰلِدُوْنَ

We granted not everlasting life to any human being before thee. If then thou shouldst die, shall they live (here) forever? (*al-Anbiyā'*, 21:35)

The fact made clear in these verses is that a more valuable or useful thing is saved. Therefore, the person most worthy of being kept alive was the Holy Prophet[sa]. Allāh says that since everlasting life was not given to the Holy Prophet[sa], it cannot be given to anyone else.

The Promised Messiah[as] writes in his Arabic couplet:

ولو انّ انسانًا یطیر الی السّماء

لکان رسول اللّٰہ اولٰی و اجدر

If any human being could attain the ability to ascend to the heavens,

Then the Holy Prophet[sa] was most suitable and deserving.

(*Barāhīn-e-Aḥmadiyya*, part 5, *Rūḥānī Khazā'in*, vol. 1, p. 332)

COUPLET 60

وَ نَبِیُّنَا حَیٌّ وَّ اِنِّیْ شَاھِدٌ
وَ قَدِ اقْتَطَفْتُ قَطَائِفَ اللُّقْیَانٖ

But our Prophet is alive, and I bear witness to his life;

And I have tasted the sweetness of being in his audience many a time.

COUPLET 61

وَرَأَيْتُ فِیْ رَیْعَانِ عُمْرِیْ وَجْهَهٗ
ثُمَّ النَّبِیُّ بِیَقْظَتِیْ لَاقَانِیْ

I saw his blessed face even when I was young,
And he also met me when I was fully awake.

The Promised Messiah[as] had seen our master, the pride of the prophets, Muḥammad Muṣṭafā[sa] many times in dreams and even in a state of *Kashf* [vision during wakefulness]. I present one quotation from his book Ā'īna'-e-Kamālāt-e-Islām, in which he has mentioned one of his dreams. It is the same book in which this Qaṣīdah is written.

اوائل ایامِ جوانی میں ایک رات مَیں نے دیکھا کہ مَیں ایک عالیشان مکان میں ہوں جو نہایت پاک اور صاف ہے اوراس میں آنحضرتؐ کا ذکر ہورہاہے میں نے لوگوں سے دریافت کیا کہ حضور کہاں تشریف فرماہیں؟ انہوں نے مجھے اس مکان کے ایک کمرے کا پتہ دیا۔ میں اسکے اندر چلا گیا اور جب میں حضور کی خدمت عالیہ میں حاظر ہوا تو حضورؐ بہت خوش ہوئے اور آپ نے مجھے سلام کا بہترین طور پر جواب دیا۔ آپؐ کا حسن وجمال اور ملاحت اور مجھ پر آپؐ کی شفقت و محبت کی نگاہ مجھے اب تک یاد ہے اور وہ

کبھی بھول نہیں سکتی۔ آپ کی محبت نے مجھے فریفتہ کر لیا اور آپؐ کے حسین و جمیل چہرہ نے مجھے اپنا گرویدہ بنالیا۔ اُس وقت آپؐ نے مجھے فرمایا کہ اے احمد! تیرے ہاتھ میں کیا چیز ہے؟ جب میں نے اپنے ہاتھ کی طرف دیکھا تو معلوم ہؤا کہ میرے ہاتھ میں ایک کتاب ہے اور وہ مجھے اپنی ہی ایک تصنیف معلوم ہوئی مَیں نے عرض کیا کہ حضور یہ میری ایک تصنیف ہے۔

In my days of youth one night I saw that I am in a glorious house which is very clean and pure and in that house there is talk of the Holy Prophet[sa]. I asked the people where the Holy Prophet[sa] is sitting and they told me about a particular room in the house and I went there. When I came face to face with Ḥuḍūr (i.e. Prophet Muḥammad[sa]), he was very pleased. He answered my salām in an excellent manner. I still remember his beauty, his kindness, and the way he looked at me with love. I can never forget it. He enchanted me with his love. I fell in love with his handsome face. He said to me at that time, "O Aḥmad, what is in your hand?" I looked at my hand and felt that I had a book in my hand, and it appeared to be a book written by me. I said to him, "Ḥuḍūr, this is my writing."

(*Ā'īna'-e-Kamālāt-e-Islām, Rūḥānī Khazā'in*, vol. 5, p. 548, translated from Arabic)

In *Barāhīn-e-Aḥmadiyya* he writes:

آنحضرت صلی اللہ علیہ وسلم نے اس کتاب کو دیکھ کر عربی زبان میں پوچھا کہ تونے اس کتاب کا کیا نام رکھا ہے۔ خاکسار نے عرض کیا کہ اس کا نام میں نے قطبی رکھا ہے۔ جس نام کی تعبیر اب اس اشتہاری کتاب کی تالیف ہونے پر یہ کھلی کہ وہ ایسی کتاب ہے کہ جو قطب ستارہ کی طرح غیر متزلزل اور مستحکم ہے جس کے کامل استحکام کو پیش کرکے دس ہزار روپیہ کا اشتہار دیا گیا ہے۔ غرض آنحضرت نے وہ کتاب مجھ سے لے لی۔ اور جب وہ کتاب حضرت مقدس نبوی کے ہاتھ میں آئی تو آنجناب کا ہاتھ مبارک لگتے ہی ایک نہایت خوش رنگ اور خوبصورت میوہ بن گئی کہ جو امرود سے مشابہ تھا مگر بقدر تربوز تھا۔ آنحضرتؐ نے جب اس میوہ کو تقسیم کرنے کے لئے قاش قاش کرنا چاہا تو اس قدر اس میں سے شہد نکلا کہ آنجناب کا ہاتھ مبارک مرفق تک شہد سے بھر گیا۔ تب ایک مردہ کہ جو دروازہ سے باہر پڑا تھا۔ آنحضرت کے معجزہ سے زندہ ہوکر اس عاجز کے پیچھے آکھڑا ہؤا اور یہ عاجز آنحضرت صلی اللہ علیہ وسلم کے سامنے کھڑا تھا جیسے ایک مستغیث حاکم کے سامنے کھڑا ہوتا ہے۔ اور آنحضرت بڑے جاہ و جلال اور حاکمانہ شان سے ایک زبردست پہلوان کی طرح کرسی پر جلوس فرما رہے تھے۔ پھر خلاصہ کلام یہ کہ ایک قاش آنحضرت صلی اللہ علیہ وسلم نے مجھ کو اس غرض سے دی کہ تا میں اس شخص کو دوں کہ جو نئے سرے زندہ ہوا۔ اور باقی تمام قاشیں میرے دامن میں ڈال دیں اور وہ ایک قاش میں نے اس نئے زندہ کو دے دی اور اس نے وہیں کھالی۔ پھر جب وہ نیا زندہ اپنی قاش کھا چکا۔ تو میں نے دیکھا کہ آنحضرت کی کرسی مبارک اپنے پہلے مکان سے بہت ہی اونچی ہوگئی۔ اور جیسے آفتاب کی کرنیں چھوٹتی ہیں

ایسا ہی آنحضرت کی پیشانی مبارک متواتر چمکنے لگی کہ جو دین اسلام کی تازگی اور ترقی کی طرف اشارت تھی۔ تب اسی نور کے مشاہدہ کرتے کرتے آنکھ کھل گئی۔ والحمد للہ علیٰ ذالک۔

The Holy Prophet[sa] asked me in Arabic when he saw this book, what name have you given this book? This humble one answered, "I have given it the name Quṭbī." The interpretation of this name has become clear when this famous book has become published42. It means that it is a book which is firm, strong and infallible just as the polar star. To prove its strength we had given a public offering of 10,000 rupees.

In short, the Holy Prophet[sa] took the book from me. As soon as this book went into the hands of the Holy Prophet, the touch of his hands made it turn into a colourful and beautiful fruit. It was like the guava fruit, but the size of a watermelon. When the Holy Prophet[sa] began to cut it, so that it could be distributed, so much juice came out of it that it began to reach his elbows. Then there was a dead body that was lying outside the door and it became alive as a miracle of the Holy Prophet[sa] and came and stood behind me. This humble one was standing in front of the Holy Prophet[sa] just as a plaintiff stands before a judge, and the Holy Prophet[sa] in a glorious and majestic manner, as a great champion, was sitting in his chair.

In short, the Holy Prophet[sa] gave me one of the slices so that I may give it to the person who had just become alive, and he put

[42] i.e., *Barāhin-e-Aḥmadiyya* (Jalāl-ud-Dīn Shams)

the remaining slices in my garment. Then I gave a slice to the revived person which he ate right there. As soon as the revived person ate that slice, I saw that the Holy Prophet'ssa chair had become elevated so that it was above the house, and just as rays come from the sun, similarly, light started emitting from the forehead of the Holy Prophetsa. This was an indication of the revival and progress of the religion of Islam. While I was still witnessing this light, I woke up.

(*Barāhīn-e-Aḥmadiyya,* Part 3, *Rūḥānī Khazā'in*, vol. 1, p. 248–249, Sub-footnote no. 1)

The Promised Messiahas also writes in his Persian Qaṣīdah which is written in his same book Ā'īna'-e-Kamālāt-e-Islām about his audience with the Holy Prophetsa:

یاد کن وقتیکه درکشفم نمودی شکل خویش
یاد کن ہم وقت دیگر کامدی مشتاق وار
یاد کن آں لطف و رحمتہا کہ بامن داشتی
واں بشارتہا کہ میدادی مرا از کردگار
یاد کن وقتے چو بنمودی بہ بیداری مرا
آں جمالے آں رخے آں صورتے رشک بہار

O my beloved, remember the time when in a kashf you showed me your face,

and do you remember that other time when you came so eagerly to see me?

Please also remember those favours and blessings that you bestowed upon me,
And remember those glad tidings that you used to give me from Allāh.

And also remember when in a state of wakening,
You showed me your beautiful and immaculate face. It was like spring time.

(*Ā'ina'-e-Kamālāt-e-Islām*, *Rūḥānī Khazā'in*, vol. 5, p. 28)

COUPLET 62

إِنِّيْ لَقَدْ أُحْيِيْتُ مِنْ إِحْيَائِهِ
وَاهًا لِإِعْجَازٍ فَمَا أَحْيَانِيْ

I am certainly among those, whom he raised to life,
What a miracle! How well he raised me to life!

In the above few couplets the fact has been revealed that the prophet who is living in his glory and sits on the throne of purity is the Holy Prophet Muḥammad[sa], and not Jesus Christ. Jesus[as] has died and the time for people to attain spirituality or purification from him has expired. However, the Holy Prophet's[sa] power of purification and spirituality is living and will perpetuate until the ends of time.

The Promised Messiah[as] has given his own example as proof of the living spirituality of the Holy Prophet[sa]. In this way he has proven the superiority of the Holy Prophet[sa] over all other prophets and simultaneously has established the truthfulness of Islam over all other religions. He writes:

اور میں اُس خدا کی قسم کھا کر کہتا ہوں جس کا نام لے کر جھوٹ بولنا سخت بدذاتی ہے کہ خدا نے مجھے میرے بزرگ واجب الاطاعت سیّدنا محمد صلی اللہ علیہ وسلم کی روحانی دائمی زندگی اور پورے جلال اور کمال کا یہ ثبوت دیا ہے کہ میں نے اسکی پیروی سے اور اسکی محبت سے آسمانی نشانوں کو اپنے اُوپر اُترتے ہوئے اور دل کو یقین کے نُور سے پُر ہوتے ہوئے پایا اور اس قدر نشانِ غیبی دیکھے کہ اُن کھُلے کھُلے نوروں کے ذریعہ سے میں نے اپنے خدا کو دیکھ لیا ہے۔

I swear in the Name of God, in Whose Name lying is a great sin, that the proof of the grandeur and ever-lasting spiritual life of my master, the Holy Prophet Muḥammad[sa], which God has given me is that by following him and by loving him I have received heavenly signs and I have seen my heart filled with the light of certainty. I have seen so many heavenly signs that through their light I have seen God Almighty Himself.

(*Tiryāqul-Qulūb, Rūḥānī Khazā'in*, vol. 15, p. 140)

He states at another place:

سو میں نے محض خدا کے فضل سے نہ اپنے کسی ہنر سے اِس نعمت سے کامل حصّہ پایا ہے جو مجھ سے پہلے نبیوں اور رسولوں اور خدا کے برگزیدوں کو دی گئی تھی۔ اور میرے لئے اِس نعمت کا پانا ممکن نہ تھا اگر میں اپنے سیّد و مولیٰ فخر الانبیاء اور خیر الوریٰ حضرت محمد مصطفٰے صلی اللہ علیہ وسلم کے راہوں کی پیروی نہ کرتا۔ سو میں نے جو کچھ پایا۔ اُس

پیروی سے پایا۔ اور میں اپنے سچے اور کامل علم سے جانتا ہوں کہ کوئی انسان بجز پیروی
اُس نبی صلی اللہ علیہ وسلم کے خدا تک نہیں پہنچ سکتا۔

Therefore, I have received these blessings only through the Grace of Allāh and not because of any of my own qualities, in the same manner that they were given to the prophets, messengers, and the people who were near to God. It was not possible for me to receive this blessing if I had not followed the path of my master, the pride of the prophets, the glorious Muḥammad Muṣṭafā[sa]. So whatever I received, I only received it through following him. I know this from factual and complete knowledge that no human being can reach God without following this Prophet[sa].

(*Ḥaqīqatul-Waḥī, Rūḥānī Khazā'in*, vol. 22, p. 64–65)

He further states:

میں سچ سچ کہتا ہوں کہ اسلام ایسے بدیہی طور پر سچاّ ہے کہ اگر تمام کفارِ رُوئے زمین دعا
کرنے کے لئے ایک طرف کھڑے ہوں اور ایک طرف صرف میں اکیلا اپنے خدا کی
جناب میں کسی امر کے لئے رجوع کروں تو خدا میری ہی تائید کرے گا مگر نہ اس لئے کہ
سب سے میں ہی بہتر ہوں بلکہ اس لئے کہ میں اُس کے رسول پر دلی صدق سے ایمان
لایا ہوں اور جانتا ہوں کہ تمام نبوتیں اُس پر ختم ہیں اور اُس کی شریعت خاتم الشرائع
ہے مگر ایک قسم کی نبوت ختم نہیں یعنی وہ نبوت جو اُس کی کامل پیروی سے ملتی ہے اور
جو اُس کے چراغ میں سے نور لیتی ہے وہ ختم نہیں کیونکہ وہ محمدی نبوت ہے یعنی اُس کا
ظِلّ ہے اور اُسی کے ذریعہ سے ہے اور اُسی کا مظہر ہے اور اُسی سے فیضیاب ہے۔ خدا

اُس شخص کا دشمن ہے جو قرآن شریف کو منسوخ کی طرح قرار دیتا ہے اور محمدی شریعت کے بر خلاف چلتا ہے اور اپنی شریعت چلانا چاہتا ہے اور آنحضرت صلی اللہ علیہ وسلم کی پیروی نہیں کرتا بلکہ آپ کچھ بننا چاہتا ہے۔ مگر خدا اُس شخص سے پیار کرتا ہے جو اس کی کتاب قرآن شریف کو اپنا دستور العمل قرار دیتا ہے اور اُس کے رسول حضرت محمد صلی اللہ علیہ وسلم کو در حقیقت خاتم الانبیاء سمجھتا ہے اور اس کے فیض کا اپنے تئیں محتاج جانتا ہے پس ایسا شخص خدا تعالیٰ کی جناب میں پیارا ہو جاتا ہے اور خدا کا پیار یہ ہے کہ اُس کو اپنی طرف کھینچتا ہے اور اُس کو اپنے مکالمہ مخاطبہ سے مشرف کرتا ہے۔

I tell you truthfully that Islam is such a true religion that if all the non-believers on planet earth stood up to pray about something on one side, and I alone pray to God on the other side, God would certainly hear my prayer, not because I am better than them, but only because I believe in His Prophet from the bottom of my heart. I know that prophethood has been finalized with him and so has his spiritual law been finalized. However, one type of prophethood has not finished and that is the one that can be achieved by following him perfectly. Therefore, since this prophethood is like a lamp that receives its light from the prophethood of Muḥammad[sa], it is part of the same prophethood and is only a part of its reflection and receives its benefits from it. God is the enemy of such a person who claims that the Holy Qur'ān has been abrogated, who acts against the Shariah of Muḥammad[sa] and wants to impose his own Shariah and does not follow the Holy Prophet Muḥammad[sa], but desires to be something himself. God loves the person who uses His book, the Holy Qur'ān, as the way of his life, and believes in the Holy Prophet Muḥammad[sa] to be the last of the prophets and considers himself to be in need of receiving benefit from the Holy Prophet Muḥammad[sa]. A person like this is loved by God and God shows His love for him by attracting him to Himself, and provides him the blessings of communication and manifests signs in his favour.

(*Chashma-e-Ma'rifat, Rūḥānī Khazā'in*, vol. 23, p. 339–340)

At another place he writes:

پادریوں کی تکذیب انتہاء تک پہنچ گئی تو خدا نے حجت محمدیہ پوری کرنے کے لئے مجھے بھیجا۔ اب کہاں ہیں پادری تا میرے مقابل پر آویں۔ میں بے وقت نہیں آیا۔ میں اُسوقت آیا کہ جب اسلام عیسائیوں کے پیروں کے نیچے کچلا گیا۔۔۔۔۔۔ اور کئی لاکھ مسلمان مرتد ہو کر خدا اور رسول کے دشمن ہو گئے۔۔۔۔۔۔ بھلا اب کوئی پادری تو میرے سامنے لاؤ جو یہ کہتا ہو کہ آنحضرت صلی اللہ علیہ وسلم نے کوئی پیشگوئی نہیں کی۔ یاد رکھو وہ زمانہ مجھ سے پہلے ہی گذر گیا اب وہ زمانہ آگیا جس میں خدا یہ ظاہر کرنا چاہتا ہے کہ وہ رسول **محمد عربیؐ** جس کو گالیاں دی گئیں۔ جس کے نام کی بے عزتی کی گئی۔ جس کی تکذیب میں بد قسمت پادریوں نے کئی لاکھ کتابیں اِس زمانہ میں لکھ کر شائع کر دیں۔ **وُہی سچا اور سچوں کا سردار ہے**۔ اُس کے قبول میں حد سے زیادہ انکار کیا گیا۔ مگر آخر اُسی رسول کو تاج عزت پہنایا گیا۔ اُس کے غلاموں اور خادموں میں سے ایک میں ہوں۔ جس سے خدا مکالمہ مخاطبہ کرتا ہے اور جس پر خدا کے غیبوں اور نشانوں کا دروازہ

کھولا گیا ہے۔ اے نادانو! تم کفر کہو یا کچھ کہو۔ تمہاری تکفیر کی اُس شخص کو کیا پرواہے جو خدا کے حکم کے موافق دین کی خدمت میں مشغول ہے اور اپنے پر خدا کی عنایات کو بارش کی طرح دیکھتا ہے۔

Since the lies of priests have become excessive, that is why God has sent me so I may provide them the proofs of the truthfulness of Muḥammad[sa]. Where are those priests? Let them come and face me. I have not come at the wrong time; I have appeared at the time when Islam had been trampled under the feet of the Christians. Several hundred thousand Muslims changed their religion and became enemies of God and His Prophet. Go ahead and bring any priest in front of me who claims that the Holy Prophet[sa] has never prophesied about anything! Remember, that time has passed before me. Now the time has come in which God will make it manifest that Prophet Muḥammad[sa] of Arabia, to whom many insults were levelled, who was slandered against, whom the unfortunate preachers wrote hundreds of thousands of books against, is the one who is truthful and is the leader of the truthful. His denial has become excessive, but in the end, the crown of respect was placed on that very prophet. I am from among his servants and slaves to whom God speaks, and upon whom the door has been opened to the signs of God and the knowledge of the unseen. O ignorant people! Call me a non-believer or whatever else, what does a person care about your remarks, who is busy serving his religion according to the commandments of God and who sees God's blessings and rewards showering upon him like rain?

(*Ḥaqīqatul-Waḥī, Rūḥānī Khazā'in*, vol. 22, p. 286)

As Allāh had provided the Promised Messiah[as] with fresh signs, as a result of his following the Holy Prophet[sa], he has used this as an argument to prove that the Holy Prophet[sa] is a living prophet, the Qur'ān is a living book and Islam is a living religion.

COUPLET 63

يَا رَبِّ صَلِّ عَلٰى نَبِيِّكَ دَائِمًا
فِيْ هٰذِهِ الدُّنْيَا وَبَعْثٍ ثَانٍ

O my Lord, always shower blessings on your Prophet,
In this world and the next.

Since in the last few couplets the Promised Messiah[as] was mentioning the favours of the Holy Prophet[sa] and the blessings that he received from Allāh, it was natural that feelings of prayer were felt in his heart. In this couplet, he prays to Allāh that He should elevate the status of the Holy Prophet[sa] in this world and the next, and that he should continually shower His blessings upon him. He has invoked *Durūd* because in fact, by sending *Durūd* on the Holy Prophet[sa] and by loving him were the means by which he received all kinds of heavenly blessings.

The following excerpt represents his remarks on one of his revelations in which Allāh asked him to send *Durūd* on the Holy Prophet[sa]:

صل علی محمد و ال محمد سید ولد ادمَ و خاتم النبیین۔ اور درود بھیج محمد اور آل محمد پر جو سردار ہے آدم کے بیٹوں کا اور خاتم الانبیاء ہے صلی اللہ علیہ وسلم۔ یہ اس بات کی طرف اشارہ ہے کہ یہ سب مراتب اور تفضلات اور عنایات اسی کے طفیل سے ہیں اور اسی سے محبت کرنے کا یہ صلہ ہے۔ سبحان اللہ اس سرور کائنات کے حضرت احدیت میں کیا ہی اعلیٰ مراتب ہیں اور کس قسم کا قرب ہے کہ اس کا محب خدا کا محبوب بن جاتا ہے اور اس کا خادم ایک دنیا کا مخدوم بنایا جاتا ہے۔۔۔۔۔۔۔اس مقام میں مجھ کو یاد آیا کہ ایک رات اس عاجز نے اس کثرت سے درود شریف پڑھا کہ دل و جان اس سے معطر ہو گیا۔ اسی رات خواب میں دیکھا کہ آب زلال کی شکل پر نور کی مشکیں اس عاجز کے مکان میں لئے آتے ہیں اور ایک نے ان میں سے کہا کہ یہ وہی برکات ہیں جو تو نے محمد کی طرف بھیجی تھی۔ صلی اللہ علیہ وآلہ وسلم۔

صل علی محمد و ال محمد سید ولد ادم و خاتم النبیین

Call down blessings on Muḥammad[sa] and the progeny of Muḥammad[sa], who is the Chief of the children of Adam, and is Khātamun-Nabiyyīn [Seal of the Prophets], may peace and blessings of Allāh be upon him. This indicates that all ranks, bounties and exaltations are through the Holy Prophet[sa] and are a reward for loving him. Holy is Allāh! How high is the rank of this prophet in the Eyes of God, and how close is he to Him that when someone loves him, he becomes the beloved of God, and his servant ends up being served by the whole world?... I recall that one night I sent Durūd in such magnitude that my heart and soul became fragrant therewith. The same night I saw in a dream that people were carrying into my house water-skins filled with divine light in the form of water and one of them said that these are the blessings that you sent on Muḥammad[sa], may peace and blessings of Allāh be upon him.

(*Barāhīn-e-Aḥmadiyya*, part 4, *Rūḥānī Khazā'in*, vol. 1, p. 597–598, Sub-footnote no.3)

COUPLET 64

يَا سَيِّدِىْ قَدْ جِئْتُ بَابَكَ لَاهِفًا
وَالْقَوْمُ بِالْإِكْفَارِ قَدْ اٰذَانِیْ

O my master, as I am oppressed, I have come to your door to seek redress,
These people slander and torment me by calling me Kāfir–a non-believer.

Imagine what would be the condition of a person who not only once but hundreds of times admits that whatever he has acquired is because of the blessings of following the Holy Prophet[sa], who believes that the Holy Prophet[sa] is a living prophet and proves that Islam is a living religion and the Qur'ān is a living book, and who spends all of his life in the service of Islam and in providing proofs of its superiority over all other religions, but he becomes rejected by the same people who claim themselves to be the followers the Holy Prophet[sa]. He gets cursed by them, is called a liar, non-believer, and is given the name *Dajjāl* [antichrist] and Satan. He is publicly maligned with hateful words among crowds of people, and everyone considers it honourable to insult him. At this point he complains to his beloved that O my beloved, these people who claim to be associated with you have rejected me and have refused to accept me. Therefore, I have come to your court for assistance.

In the time of the Promised Messiah[as] many renowned scholars issued *fatāwā* [religious verdicts] in 1891 and the following are a few excerpts from them:

Maulawī Syed Nadhīr Ḥusain and many other scholars wrote together as follows:

> Mirza Qādiānī is one of the thirty Dajjāls mentioned in the ḥadīth, his followers are the children of Dajjāl. Muslims must stay away from this type of Dajjāl and must not join them in performing any religious matters as they normally would with other Muslims. Muslims should not sit with him nor accept his invitation, should not say prayers behind him, and must not perform his funeral prayer... He and people like him are thieves of religion. They are from Dajjāl, they are liars, they are accursed, they are satans... There is no doubt that this Qādiānī is a non-believer and an apostate... He is a very big Dajjāl and is out of the pale of Islam, and is an infidel and is of bad character..., has the lowest morals and is an enemy of God... Any person who doubts in his being on the wrong path is just as wrong himself and is himself a Kāfir rather Akfar [the greatest disbeliever]... He is worse than the Satan that is playing with him and he must not be allowed to be buried in a Muslim cemetery... He is an enemy of the prophets and God is his enemy... Any person who has the

same beliefs as of Qādiānī is an outcast. Mirza Qādiānī is a Dajjāl and actually, the leader of Dajjāls. Their women's marriages have been nullified and anyone is free to marry them.

(*Fatwā of the scholars of India and Arabia and Fatwā by 'ulamā of Ludhiana,* published in Ishā'ātus-Sunnah, vol. 13, no.6–7 / *Pāk-o-Hind kay 'Ulamā'-e-Islām Kā Awwalīn Muttafiqqah Fatwā,* by Muḥammad Ḥusain Batālawī, Dārud-Da'watis-Salafiyyah, Lahore 1986)

Maulawī Muḥammad Ḥusain Batalawī hurled a number of insults upon him, the following being examples: The hidden enemy of Islam, Musailamah the second, *Dajjāl* of our times, fortune teller, cunning liar, accursed, faithless, subject of a thousand curses, atheist, bigger fool than all the fools of the world, his God is Satan, a Jew, adulterer, drunkard, the one who eats *Ḥarām* and his followers without morals, etc.

(*Ishā'atus-Sunnah,* vol. 14, no.1 year 1891, article entitled, *'Qādiānī Kay Āsmānī Faiṣalah Kī Tarmīm*)

In the following Persian couplets the Promised Messiah[as] complains about this rejection addressing the Holy Prophet[sa]:

آنچہ مارا از دو شیخ شوخ آزارے رسید

یارسول اللہ بپرس از عالم ذو الاقتدار

حال ماؤ شوخی ایں ہر دو شیخ بدزباں
جملہ میداند خدائے حال دان و بردبار
نام من دجال وضال و کافرے بنہادہ اند
نیست اندر زعم شاں چوں من پلیدو زشت وخوار
ہیچ کس رابرمن مظلوم و غمگیں دل نسوخت
جز تو کاندر خو ابہار رحمت نمودی بار بار

Meaning, O Prophet of Allāh, inquire of the All-Knowing Allāh, with respect to the pain we have received from these two maulawīs (Maulawī Nadhīr Ḥusain Dehlwī, and Muḥammad Ḥusain Batālawī). My condition and the mischief of these two slanderous people is apparent to my Lord. They have named me Dajjāl and a non-believer. In their opinion there is no other who is evil, filthy and shameless. Nobody's heart bled for me, who is in grief and is oppressed, except You who have time after time, favoured me through dreams.

(*Ā'īna'-e-Kamālāt-e-Islām*, *Rūḥānī Khazā'in*, vol. 5, p. 28)

COUPLET 65

يَفْرِىْ سِهَامُكَ قَلْبَ كُلِّ مُحَارِبٍ
وَيَشُجُّ عَزْمُكَ هَامَةَ الثُّعْبَانِ

Your arrows pierce the heart of all enemies,
And your firm resolve crushes the head of the serpent.

In this couplet he explains the reason for complaining to the Holy Prophet[sa], for the relationship between the Holy Prophet[sa] and Allāh is such that his enemy cannot escape punishment. If the people, who slander me as a non-believer and an enemy of Allāh, are truthful then I will be destroyed. On the other hand, if they are wrong in rejecting me and I am in fact your true lover, then they cannot go unpunished. In fact, the latter is exactly how events transpired.

Today you cannot find anyone who claims to be a follower of these scholars. They disappeared from the earth in such a manner that no trace of them was left behind. Maulawī Muḥammad Ḥusain Batālawī, who was the instigator of gathering the verdict and travelled from city to city in India, visiting scholars of Islam, was sorely humiliated by God. Ḥaḍrat Khalīfatul-Masīḥ II writes in *Tafsīr-e-Kabīr*:

> Once he said with great pride that I elevated Mirzā Ṣāḥib and I am the one who will bring him down, but after that, let alone

> bringing Mirzā Ṣāḥib down, he brought himself down. As a matter of fact, his two sons ran away from his house and came to me in Qadian. They said to me that their father has no conscience and he tells them to go and join an orphanage. He beats us all the time and forces us to do menial chores. We simply do not want to live with him any longer. I put both of them on allowance and provided them education in Qadian. When Maulawī Muḥammad Ḥusain discovered this he sent me a message that this was a big disgrace for him and that his sons should be removed from Qadian. I responded that it was not possible that they come to me for help and I deny them. Afterwards, both of them became Ahmadis, but later on Maulawī Ṣāḥib came and pressured them into leaving Qadian. However, it was apparent that his treatment with them was so extreme that one of them died and the other became a Christian. He is still alive and does business in the state of Maisur.
>
> (*Tafsīr-e-Kabīr*, vol. 8, part. 3, p. 451)

At the time they issued the verdict of disbelief against the Promised Messiah[as], all these scholars of Islam enjoyed glory and prestige. However, what happened from that point on until their death is apparent to the whole world. Even the enemies of Aḥmadiyyat admitted that all their efforts against this Jamā'at were wasted. On the other hand, Allāh gave respect to the Promised Messiah[as] and made his name famous and gave his Jamā'at remarkable progress. His Jamā'at exists in every corner of the world today. His missions can be found in Washington, Chicago, and in many other states and cities, in London, and even in many European countries, as well as Africa and many cities of Asia. This Jamā'at continues to progress by the Grace of Allāh day by day.

COUPLET 66

لِلّٰهِ دَرُّكَ يَا إِمَامَ الْعَالَمِ
أَنْتَ السَّبُوْقُ وَ سَيِّدُ الشُّجْعَانِ

Bravo! O leader of the world!
You rank above all, the bravest of the brave.

COUPLET 67

اُنْظُرْ إِلَيَّ بِـرَحْـمَةٍ وَّ تَحَنُّنٍ
يَا سَيِّدِىْ أَنَا أَحْقَرُ الْغِلْمَانِ

Look at me with mercy and grace,
O my master, I am your most humble servant.

COUPLET 68

يَاحِبِّ إِنَّكَ قَدْ دَخَلْتَ مَحَبَّةً
فِي مُهْجَتِي وَ مَدَارِكِي وَجَنَانِي

O my beloved, my adoration for you has penetrated into my blood, heart, soul and body.

This couplet describes extreme love and it becomes apparent that the love of the Promised Messiah[as] was natural, comprehensive, and of the highest quality, and not mere superficiality. It seems that the Holy Prophet[sa] had been absorbed in the heart, the soul, and in every particle of his body. The truth is that when a person truly loves a person, he becomes absolved in his beloved. He draws a picture of his beloved in himself in a manner as if he has either drank him or eaten him, and has in fact made him a part of his body.

This was the condition of the love of the Promised Messiah[as] and this was the love that Allāh cherished so much that He appointed him to revive His religion. The Promised Messiah[as] states:

> Once I received a revelation that the angels were in strife (arguing with one another). They were having contentions because Allāh's Will was at its height to revive His religion, but the appointed person had not been disclosed to the angels. During this time I saw in a dream that people are searching for this reviver and a person came up to me and said this is the person who loves the

Prophet of Allāh. These words meant that the primary requirement for this candidate is the love of the Prophet and my person is proven to have it.

(*Barāhīn-e-Aḥmadiyya*, part 4, *Rūḥānī Khazā'in*, vol. 1, p. 598, sub-footnote no. 3)

In another Arabic Qaṣīdah he writes:

انت الّذی شغف الجنان محبة

انت الّذی کالروح فی حوبائی

انت الّذی بودادہ و بحبّہ

ایّدتُ بالالهام و الالقاءِ

You are the one in whose love my heart is completely absorbed.

You are like the soul in my body.

You are the one because of whose love and affection

I have been provided revelation and nearness to Allāh.

(*Anjām-e-Ātham, Rūḥānī Khazā'in*, vol. 11, p. 280)

COUPLET 69

مِنْ ذِكْرِ وَجْهِكَ يَا حَدِيْقَةَ بَهْجَتِيْ
لَمْ أَخْلُ فِيْ لَحْظٍ وَّلَا فِيْ اٰنٍ

O you my garden of delight, you live in my memory all the time,
I see your face every moment of my life.

In this couplet just as the Arabic saying goes من احبّ شيأً اكثر ذكرهٗ that a person talks much about the one he loves, he has expressed the intensity of his love for the Holy Prophet[sa] of Islam.

COUPLET 70

جِسْمِيْ يَطِيْرُ إِلَيْكَ مِنْ شَوْقٍ عَلَا
يَا لَيْتَ كَانَتْ قُوَّةُ الطَّيَرَانِ

My body yearns to fly towards you out of love;
Would that I had the power to fly!

In this couplet the writer of this Qaṣīdah has, in a beautiful manner, explained the intensity of his love and its perfection. He says that although my beloved and I are like one soul with two hearts, my physical heart, out of its intensity of love, wants to fly towards you so it can unite with your heart and become one. He wishes that he could fly. He has stated the same idea in one of his Persian poems:

ے پریدم سوئے کوئے او مدام
من اگر ے داشتم بال و پرے

If I had wings I would incessantly fly towards him.
(*Barāhīn-e-Aḥmadiyya*, part 1, *Rūḥānī Khazā'in*, vol. 1, p. 19)

A BEAUTIFUL FINISH

The last two couplets of this Qaṣīdah are the best example of a beautiful finish. In the beginning of the Qaṣīdah he states the qualities and the excellent accomplishments of his beloved or the reasons for his love, and at the end he mentions his everlasting love for him. He ended his Qaṣīdah in a manner illustrating that every moment of his life was spent in the love of the Holy Prophet[sa]. He was flying through the endless space of the world of love, which has no boundaries.

AN ADMISSION

It was not possible to explain in this brief explanation of the Qaṣīdah all the qualities and excellences that are mentioned in this Qaṣīdah. Therefore, I must admit that I have not been able to give its proper due, nor is it possible to do it. As much as I have written is only the result of Allāh's favour that he allowed me to write during my illness.

A FINAL WORD

What I want to write now is that the essence of Islam is *Kalimah Ṭayyibah* [First pillar of Islām]:

لا الٰہ الا اللہ محمّد الرسول اللہ

In other words, this refers to the Oneness of God and prophethood of Muḥammad[sa]. The first part of the *Kalimah* revolves around the Oneness of Allāh. In the manner that the Holy Prophet[sa] emphasized the Oneness of God, through his words and actions, displayed the Glory of the One God in a manner unparalleled by any other prophet. The Holy Prophet[sa] would mention Allāh's name when he was eating, drinking, travelling, being awake, sleeping, or putting on clothes. He would see the Glory of his Lord in the water falling from the falls, the lightning, and the thunder of the clouds, the storms, rains, floods, rivers, the ocean tides, the earthquakes and shaking of mountains. It was for the sake of establishing the Oneness of God that the entire Peninsula of Arabia became his enemy. He gave such sacrifice in establishing the Unity of God, that Allāh Himself gave witness that his prayers, sacrifices, his life and his death – thus, everything that was associated to him was for the sake of the God of all the worlds. On the other hand, his enemies admitted that Muḥammad[sa] is madly in love with his Lord.

The second part of the *Kalimah*, refers to the prophethood of Muḥammad[sa] and includes the name Muḥammad[sa], meaning the one who is praised extensively. The truth that was hidden in this part was to be fulfilled in our time when the priests, western philosophers and Hindu Aryas attacked the name of the Holy Prophet[sa] and hurled various insults at him. Allāh appointed the spiritual son of Muḥammad[sa], Ḥaḍrat Mirzā Ghulām Aḥmad[as], the writer of the Qaṣīdah, to praise Muḥammad[sa] and confront his enemies so the entire world could witness how glorious and praiseworthy Allāh had made the Holy Prophet[sa]. This was to prove to the whole world that Muḥammad[sa] is its benefactor and to manifest the countless advantages there are tied to accepting and following him. This was to establish that the whole world should see that nearness to God, which is essential for the success in the next world, could only be achieved by following the Holy Prophet[sa]. This was to establish that the world must understand that the Holy Prophet[sa] was a blessing for mankind and the whole world would praise him, and be filled by his praise just as much as the waters fill the oceans.

The founder of the Ahmadiyya Muslim Community in explaining the reason for his advent writes in his book *Tiryāqul-Qulūb*:

> O people who live upon the earth, and all those human souls living in the east and the west, I invite you with my full power that now the only true religion on earth is Islam, and the Only True God is the God that the Qur'ān has explained, and the prophet with everlasting spiritual light and glory, and the one who sits on the throne of purity, is Ḥaḍrat Muḥammad, Muṣṭafā[sa] [the

Chosen One], may peace and blessing of Allāh be upon him. The proof of his spiritual life and his sacred glory is that by following him and loving him we can receive the Holy Spirit, communication with our God, and can experience heavenly signs.

(*Tiryāqul-Qulūb, Rūḥānī Khazā'in*, vol. 15, p. 141)

اللهم صلّ علی محمدٍ وعلیٰ آل محمدٍ کما صلیت علیٰ ابراھیم و علیٰ آل ابراھیم انک حمیدٌ مجیدٌ۔ اللھم بارک علیٰ محمدٍ وعلیٰ آل محمدٍ کما بارکت علیٰ ابراھیم و علیٰ آل ابراھیم انک حمیدٌ مجیدٌ۔

Humbly,
Jalāl-ud-Dīn Shams
Quetta, Pakistan
8 September 1956

QAṢĪDAH[1]

قصيدة

القرآن العظیم و اصحاب النبی الکریم

The Qaṣīdah which is being presented below is due to the blessings of the fruits of the Qaṣīdah, written by the Promised Messiah[as], for which I have written this commentary.

(*A humble one, Jalāl-ud-Dīn Shams*)

---

[1] I wrote this Qaṣīdah in November 1951 and it was published in *Al-Faḍl* (Special Jalsah Sālānah Edition) and in *al-Furqān* (December, 1951 edition)

إن شئتَ بحرَ العلمِ و العِرفانِ

فاقرأ كِتابَ اللهِ بِالإمعانِ

If you seek an ocean of knowledge and understanding
Then read Allāh's book attentively.

سِفرٌ كريمٌ كاملٌ و مكملٌ

فردٌ و لَم يوجد له من ثانی

It is a priceless book, comprehensive and perfect,
with none like unto it.

نُورٌ مُبينٌ ساطعٌ مِن رّبِّنا

ضَوءٌ مُضیءٌ سائرَ البُلدانِ

It is a light, which is very high, from our Lord,
And of such intensity that it can illuminate all of the cities.

تَاجُ الهدیٰ فَخرُ الشرائع کله

و الحق کل الخیر فی القرآنِ

It is the crown of guidance and the pride of all Shariahs,
And the fact is that everything good is found in the Holy Qur'ān.

كالسمط تبدوا ايهٔ منظومةٌ

الفاظهٔ كالدّرّ فی اللمعانِ

Its verses are like a pearl necklace
And each word glitters like a real pearl.

آياتهٔ تُلقی اذا دبّرتها

بحر الحقائقِ منبع العرفانِ

If you ponder and reflect upon its verses,
You will discover an ocean of evidence and understanding.

فی ليلةٍ ظُلماءَ كان نزولهٔ

ارخت سدول الغيّ والطغيانِ

It was revealed in a dark time,
When wickedness and erring ways were rampant.

العربُ من ظلمٍ و من جهلٍ غَدَتْ

مِثل السِباع بهيكل الانسانِ

The Arabs were like animals in the shape of human beings because of their ignorance and cruelty.

كانتْ كخافيةِ الغُدافِ قُلُوبُهُم

مِن كثرتِ الاٰثامِ و العِصْيانِ

With sins and rejecting commandments, their hearts had become black like the wings of a crow.

كانوا كغرقیٰ فی هواءِ نفوسهم

واللهوا بِالنُّدماءِ و النسوانِ

They were distracted in the pleasures of drinking, women, and satisfying their worldly desires.

صاروا كانعامٍ كثيرٌ منهم

مذكورةٌ فی سورةِ الفرقانِ

They had actually become like the cattle referenced in Surah Furqan.

زال العمی بعد الهُدیٰ من قلبهم

وتشبّتوا بِالقسطِ والميزانِ

After they received guidance, the blindness of their hearts disappeared,

And they established justice and equality in a great manner.

نقّوا بماءِ الوحی جذرَ جنابِهِم

مِن رِجس اَوثانٍ و مِن اضغانِ

They took the water of revelation and cleaned the filth of their idols, and their malice.

فاقوا الوریٰ دنیا و دینًا کُلُّهُمْ

لما اتَوا بِاَوامِرِ القُرآنِ

When they acted upon the commandments of the Qur'ān they achieved superiority in the religious and secular world over all others.

واطّهّروا حتّٰی تبرّأ کُلُّهُمْ

مِن کل نوعٍ الذنبِ والعصیانِ

They purified themselves to the extent that,
Every one of them became pure of all kinds of sin.

هُم جاهدوا الکفّار طول نهارهم

واللیلَ باتوا طالبِي الغُفرنِ

In the daytime they fought with non-believers and consumed their nights in seeking forgiveness from Allāh.

زكّوا نفوسهم فكان فُؤادُهُمْ

كَالكَوْكبِ الدُّرّيِ في اللمعانِ

They purified themselves in such a way that their hearts became like glittering stars.

حازوا المَكارمَ والفضائلَ جُمّةً

ما حازها جيلٌ مِنَ الْانسانِ

They toiled to receive God's blessings to an
extent that no other group was capable.

وَاستمسكوا بالذكر حتّٰى جاءَهُم

وحيٌ يُبشرهم مِنَ الرحمن

They embraced the Qur'ān with such intensity that Allāh gave them glad tidings.

آَجْرٌ ومَغْفِرَةٌ لهم مِنْ رَّبهم

طُوبى لهُم فَضْلاً من المنّانِ

Announcing that for them is forgiveness and reward from Allāh; they will receive all varieties of grace.

نالوا مِنَ الرَّحمٰنِ کُلَّ کرامةٍ

فازوا بِفَضلِ اللہ الرضوانِ

They received all kinds of honour from their God and Allāh was pleased with them and granted them favours.

طاروا بِاَمرِ نبیھم فی العالمِ

مِثلِ الحمائمِ حاملی القرآنِ

They followed the orders of their prophet, picked up the Holy Qur'ān and dispersed throughout the world as doves fly everywhere.

ربّی النبیُ محمدٌ اصحابہٗ

بِتحننٍ کالاُمِّ للولدانِ

The Holy Prophet Muḥammad[sa] *instructed his companions with such love and affection, just as a mother raises her children.*

ھُم اِقتدوا بِمحمدٍ خیرِ الوریٰ

عینِ الھُدیٰ ذِی الحُسن والاحسانِ

They followed Muḥammad[sa] *who had the best morals, was the source of guidance, and was a blessing.*

يا ربِّ صلِّ على النبي محمدٍ

خيرِ الخلائقِ مهبطِ القرآنِ

O my Lord, send Durūd on Muḥammad[sa] *who is superior and better than all creations, upon whom the Qur'ān was revealed.*

تمتْ بِالخَيْرِ

www.ingramcontent.com/pod-product-compliance
Lightning Source LLC
Chambersburg PA
CBHW071610080526
44588CB00010B/1085
* 9 7 8 1 8 4 8 8 0 0 9 0 8 *